How Brain Science
and the Bible
Help Parents Raise
Resilient Children

signals

CHERILYN ORR

with Katherine Bennett, Rebecca Dougan,
Ryland Frank, Emily Ham,
and Rachel Jones

FOCUS
ON THE FAMILY.

A Focus on the Family Resource
Published by Tyndale House Publishers

Table of Contents

Introduction

How can I write a book about parenting?

I sometimes still ask myself that question, or a version of it. I know how imperfect I am at this job. I'm frequently fatigued and often feel like a total failure as I try to guide my kids toward wisdom and resilience. There have been times when I wasn't sure I had the physical, emotional, or mental strength to finish the day, much less help other parents understand how to get through *their* days.

Why would anyone want to hear what I have to say?

I expressed my doubts to my husband as I was considering this project. He agreed that we've faced some big challenges in our family, but that it was these trials that gave me the ability to help other parents. "You have lived it," he said. "You can speak into other parents' lives not because you are perfect or make every decision perfectly, but because you understand the challenges so well."

You have lived it. We have indeed. These days, we usually have ten children sitting around our dinner table at night: seven kids of our own—four of whom we've adopted—and a few other foster children we've brought under our roof until the situation improves for them elsewhere. Several of the children we've welcomed into

1

our home have faced special academic and behavioral challenges; a few others have experienced significant trauma. And we've done all of this while living overseas outside the comforts of our own culture. As my husband reminded me, our family life is a lot more complicated than what many people our age experience—raising a couple of kids in a big home in the suburbs. Whether through our family life or our ministry, there aren't many parenting challenges we haven't faced.

Being a mom to these kids constantly reminds me that family life is a place for growth—for kids, obviously, but also for parents. And I have seen much growth in my parenting strategies. Early on, I used the sorts of tactics my own parents used as I was growing up. If you're around my age, you may know what I'm talking about: a sort of fear-based system of expectations enforced with punishment. Obey the rules or reap the consequences.

Don't get me wrong: My mom and dad were good parents in the sense that they wanted what was best for my siblings and me. They did what they could with what they had, and I remember with fondness their wisdom, love, and good intentions. But I also recognize that most moms and dads of that generation didn't have the resources and understanding of science and childhood development that we are fortunate to have today.

So that's another reason I can help parents: I've witnessed firsthand how helpful a parenting approach that fuses scientific research and biblical wisdom can help us do our jobs better. These insights have taught me the importance of adjusting my parenting strategies to fit the reality of how kids and parents best function together.

The strategies we'll be looking at are likely not major departures from your philosophy of parenting. We all love our kids and want to guide them toward making good decisions that will help them be successful in life. But it is helpful to align our tactics with how kids are functioning in the heat of the moment. That is my goal with this book: to help parents recognize how and when children and parents best function, based on how God made us.

Of course, changing one's parenting strategy isn't ever very easy. You may be changing habits that have become deeply entrenched. It's difficult, for example, to unlearn the habit of instantly and harshly reacting to misbehavior and then replace that habit with a more intentional, growth-focused response. It's hard work, and these decisions can take a lot of repetition before they become a natural part of you. But understanding how kids are *built*—how the state of a child's brain influences his or her behavior and decision-making ability in times of stress or peace—is an incredibly powerful tool to have at your disposal.

●　●　●

So, what is this tool and how can I get it? To answer that, let's briefly jump back to the spring of 2011. I was in one of those "feeling absolutely overwhelmed" phases of parenting. Traveling as a family tends to amplify those feelings. There were nine of us at the time, and we were in the middle of a family road trip across two countries. All of us, in a van, for hours on end. There were some difficult moments.

We stopped to spend a couple days at my friend Marilyn's house. Marilyn specializes in child development, so many of our conversations naturally turned to parenting and our work with children who had experienced trauma. I told her about the challenges of my adopted children, including one extremely spirited child who always seemed to have a will that was directly opposed to mine. Our home school lesson times were especially trying, often disintegrating into full-throated temper tantrums (from my daughter, not me). I couldn't figure out what I was doing wrong. I was trying to make the lessons easy to understand and within each child's skill level. I also kept school on a routine as much as possible, knowing that kids best function when the day's events are predictable. Even on our road trip, we stuck to a basic learning schedule. But it seemed that a full-on battle ensued every day, especially with this one daughter.

I invited Marilyn to join our school time the next morning. Things started out fine. The children were fed and seemed ready to focus on their assignments. And the task that morning was pretty simple and low-key. I asked my kids to draw and color a picture about something interesting or enjoyable they'd experienced so far on our trip. Below the picture, they were to print a sentence describing the scene.

It wasn't long before my spirited little girl started fussing, then complaining, then refusing to start on her picture. I tried to encourage her, telling her that she could easily do this small, fun project, and that if she could just focus for a short time, she could be back to playing before she knew it. But she wasn't interested. Tensions rose, and within a few minutes she was totally overwhelmed. She was soon throwing herself on the floor, screaming and thrashing in a typical tantrum style. I stood back a little, pleading with my girl to come back to the table. We'd been in this situation many times before, and I knew that this behavior could go on for quite some time, with no schoolwork getting done.

As Marilyn reminded me, this was not typical or healthy behavior for a six-year-old child. My friend leaned close to me and asked if she could try something that might help, and I nodded my approval. I was not prepared for the transformation in behavior my friend could achieve.

Marilyn laid on the floor next to my daughter, speaking quietly to her. Within a short time—fifteen minutes or so—my daughter was back up and sitting at the table, working on her picture. It was an amazing turnaround, and in such a short time. This was something that would normally have taken me an hour or more to accomplish.

Of course, I wanted to know what Marilyn had done, and she began explaining to me some of the basic parenting concepts known in this book as the Stoplight Approach. Marilyn explained the importance of recognizing which "mode" a child's brain was in and using that understanding to guide our interactions and instructions. She used the simple metaphor of a stoplight's three colors to explain the workings of a child's brain and the very different needs the child has when operating in each of these phases.

Marilyn introduced me to cutting-edge brain research by neuroscience researcher Dr. Bruce Perry. In his research, Dr. Perry has shown that one's intelligence and capacity for learning drops significantly when in a state of duress. Perry has shown that, when stressed, a child's practical intelligence can drop as much as fifty percent. This weakened state directly influences a child's ability to comprehend reasonable, logical instructions. So the goal should be to move into another mode—to satisfy the needs a child's brain has in one mode and shift into a phase that better accommodates learning and growth.

Marilyn's knowledge of this area of brain science sparked a passion inside me. I had just witnessed it applied effectively in a stressful parenting scenario, and I wanted to know how I could do it myself and teach others to do the same. And so, I became a student of one of the most fascinating aspects of God's creation: the human brain. I spent many thousands of hours studying and learning from top neuroscientists, researchers, and trauma specialists from around the world.

As a parent, I was especially interested in the connection between modern brain research and child development. I recognized that there was great value in learning a little more about how God created our brains and emotions to function and how that deeper understanding can greatly improve the effectiveness of our parenting. Yes, life is messy and imperfect, but God doesn't wait for us to have our lives together before He can use us. In our weakness, He is strong!

● ● ●

The Stoplight Approach is a tool that can be used to foster the spiritual formation of our children, as we are called to love God, love others, and be a witness as we go into all the world to share His love.

As I make mistakes, I can understand where I went wrong. When I do mess up, I know I can make repairs and reconnect with my children so that we grow together. The Stoplight Approach is a philosophy, not a program, giving me the framework within which to develop my own emotional intelligence and the spiritual formation of my family. It helps me grow my self-awareness and enables me to regulate my emotions while giving me the tools to parent my children in a way that meets their need for discipline, love, and safety. It is a way of seeing myself and others through the lens of brain science, and it can change the most challenging relationship into a positive connection. This book is not meant to make any of us feel guilty for the way we have parented but to give insight so that we can work toward a scientifically based parenting approach.

Alison Gopnik uses a helpful metaphor in her book, *The Gardener and the Carpenter*. She explains that parents should be like gardeners, not carpenters. Our children are not like blocks of wood that we have full control over their final form. No, children are more like flowers, each beautiful and unique. We provide an environment for growth, the best we possibly can, but the outcome is still in part determined by who the child is and the choices they make.[1]

Though there are many styles of parenting, the Stoplight Approach gives parents a style of parenting within the framework of three simple colors: Red, Yellow, and Green. How do you get your home from chaotic to peaceful, from aggressive to calm, from Red to Green? Join me on a journey to learn and understand what it means to be a Stoplight parent and how it can not only change your life and the entire atmosphere of your home but ultimately help your children grow into connected adults who engage in caring communities and work toward a kinder world.

CHAPTER 1

The Brain in Stoplight

I's six in the morning, back when we were living in Uganda. I feel someone's eyes staring at me while I sleep. As I slowly wake up, I see my seven-year-old son Peter gazing at me from beside the bed. "Mommy," he says sweetly. "It's morning and I'm hungry!"

I roll over and remember that Rachel, my six-year-old daughter, had a nightmare the night before. She is now lying in such a way that her feet are poking me in the ribs. I slowly sit up to see Gordon, our six-year-old foster child who is deaf and has cerebral palsy, now wide awake. Somehow, he has also crept into the bed. I can't remember why.

"Okay, I'll be down in a minute," I say to Peter. Needless to say, I could probably use a bit more sleep.

I notice that the bedroom light is on and remember there was a rat in my room last night, and I was too scared to sleep in the dark. *Wonder where that thing went.*

I hear Peter jumping down the stairs. Instead of waiting for me, he decides to be a big boy and pour his own cereal. This is then followed by him spilling milk across the counter and onto the floor. By this point, Gordon has followed after him and is now standing in a puddle of milk. Of course, I haven't discovered any of this yet because I'm still trying to pull myself out of bed.

My husband is usually the first one up and on duty in the morning, but he is away on an overnight business trip and can't do the breakfast routine. I am not a morning person by nature, but this morning is different. Time to get up and put on my Mummy hat.

I wake up Rachel and walk downstairs to start the day. Questions start filling my mind. *Why didn't I make the kids' lunches last night? Do we have any bread for sandwiches? I don't think so. Guess we're making pancakes this morning.*

And then I see milk all over the kitchen floor. *Well, no pancakes either. Guess we're using yogurt instead.*

"Who peed on my volleyball uniform?" says Joshua, my sixteen-year-old son, walking into the kitchen. He is livid, holding up a jersey that is dripping wet. I glance around the room, trying to collect some information. I quickly deduce that the responsible party probably wasn't Thomas, my fourteen-year-old son, or Robert, my seventeen-year-old nephew. It also probably wasn't any of the girls, who sleep in a separate room.

My attention turns to Peter, who is now trying to mop up the spilled milk. "Joshua said I could sleep in his bed last night, and he left his uniform on the bed," Peter admits, "and I had an accident in the middle of the night."

Joshua sniffs the jersey. "I have a game today! I can't play with this!"

I grab the uniform and assure him that I will have his uniform cleaned and at school by the time his game starts. Did I mention the power just went out? Hand washing it is!

It's now past seven o'clock, and the kids leave for school in less than an hour. I discover that Beth, one of my ten-year-old daughters, didn't finish her homework. Jessica, my other ten-year-old daughter, is still in bed. And Rachel is now crying because she can't find her lunch box.

Oh, right. I still need to make some lunches.

Gordon has decided to dress himself and is now working toward emptying every cabinet in the bedroom. Thomas casually informs me that the cat has pooped in the sock basket. Joshua is about to walk out the door with or without his little siblings, because he doesn't want to be late for school. While all this goes on, I am frantically signing school forms, brushing hair, flipping pancakes, and yelling at anyone who gets in my way.

Welcome to my life.

• • •

Does the chaos of life ever totally stress you out? Ever feel like you're stuck on a roller coaster and you've completely lost control of where you're going? How about when your voice seems stuck on "yell" because nobody is listening to you?

As parents, we all emotionally react (and sometimes overreact) to the fury of family activity. Sometimes those reactions make those we love feel safe, and sometimes they make them feel unsafe. There are good days and bad days, moments we are proud of, and moments we'd like to take another swing at.

You probably don't consider very often how your brain is contributing to your responses to your family. We can't see the brain, of course, but it does send clear signals to us and to those around us. Like a traffic light sending signals for drivers to proceed, clear the intersection, or stop, our brains direct their own sort of traffic, guiding our emotions and behaviors, which in turn send their own signals to those around us. The Stoplight

Approach teaches parents how to understand and read these signals, helping grow our awareness of our own and our child's emotions, and helping us to know what kind of actions to take based on the signal sent.

My Brain Does What?

If you had to pick which organ in your body was the most important, the brain would definitely make the short list. Without a brain, you wouldn't be . . . well, *you*. The brain is a sort of central computer for human operations. It directs our actions and reactions. It gives us thoughts and emotions and allows us to have memories. All of that functionality makes the brain the most complex organ in the human body. It is so complex that brain scientists still don't understand everything about it.

What a marvel of creation our brains are! Seeking to understand the brain and how it works is a way of honoring God because it honors how He made us. There's so much to discover! And brain scientists have learned quite a lot about this most important organ.

One thing research shows us is that the human brain is wired for relationship. People have a hardwired need to be around other people, to interact and share life with each other. In his book *Social Intelligence*, Daniel Goleman describes this as a sort of "neural ballet" that connects human brains. "Neuroscience has discovered that our brain's very design makes it sociable, inexorably drawn into an intimate brain-to-brain linkup whenever we engage with another person," Goleman writes.[1]

For Christians, these kinds of discoveries are no surprise. Humans are made in the image of a relational God—one who has been in a kind of perfect relationship with Himself for all eternity as Father, Son, and Holy Spirit. So it's no surprise that when God made humans in His image, He gave us brains that are wired to seek and support relational connection. We are relational because our Creator is relational. Later, we'll look more closely at how humanity's hardwiring for relational connection applies to parenting.

Another aspect of the brain that has recently received a lot of study and attention is *neuroplasticity*, the brain's ability to restructure itself in response to different sensory experiences. Your brain can change dramatically over time depending on the stimuli you receive and the habits you develop. And this changing, learning quality of the brain can be utilized for positive and negative purposes. For example, practicing a musical or artistic skill until it feels automatic is neuroplasticity at work. But the same is true of a bad habit: The brain gets accustomed to a certain pattern of behavior, and it can be difficult to break free from the pattern.

As with the brain's relational wiring mentioned above, we must also consider the brain's neuroplastic nature when discussing effective parenting. Our actions and reactions directly influence the way our children's brains develop and can have both positive and negative effects on their lives. A pattern of interactions with a child will cause them to expect such interactions in the future and adjust accordingly.

Given the background of many kids that I've worked with, I've become very interested in the brain's capacity to change itself. Can this capacity for change help heal a child who has experienced trauma? Scientists have shown that this, indeed, is the case. Just like a broken arm can be mended if dealt with correctly or cause a lifetime of disability and pain if it is not, so too our interactions with our children can heal or disable. Yes, damage to the brain in the early years can have long-term effects, but the brain is always capable of change. New and healthier patterns can still influence a hurting brain. There is always hope.

Signals along the Road

Like traffic signs along a road, our brain is continually sending signals to help us react and respond to our environment. Unfortunately, we don't always recognize what those signals mean. And, as on the roadway, people can get hurt when we don't respect or understand the signs that help us know where to go and how to proceed.

To learn how to respect these signals, it's important that we understand some basics about the structure of the human brain. As mentioned earlier, the human brain is incredibly complex, and as scientists have studied the major areas, they've defined and divided them further based on specific functions and focuses. But for our purposes, we'll look at three main areas of the brain.

The **neocortex**, which is also called the neopallium or the isocortex, is often described as the "thinking brain" or "rational brain." As those words suggest, this part of the brain is a high-level thinker. It's very logical and thoughtful. It's involved in remembering the past in order to make decisions about the future. If your son is planning for a big school project, analyzing the different steps with deadlines and follow-up processes, he will be relying extensively on his neocortex.

In the stoplight metaphor for the brain, let's think of the neocortex and its state of thinking as the green light mode. Imagine that the neocortex is saying, "Go! It is safe to proceed at full speed." While we don't really activate or deactivate different parts of our brain, we do "shift" states to use different parts of our brain in a deeper way as our needs are met and we focus on other tasks. When we shift to the green light state, we are more capable of using our advanced thinking and reasoning abilities to address a situation.

The **limbic system**, often described as the "feeling brain," is the emotional and social-relational section of the brain. When we feel loved, supported, and encouraged for doing something well, we're using this system, and that's also true when we feel disrespected, embarrassed, or angry.

Under the Stoplight Approach, let's think of the limbic system as a yellow light. You can imagine it saying, "Be cautious! Slow down to stop or clear the intersection right away!" When in yellow light mode, it can be difficult to see facts and reason because our feelings and emotions may be clouding the situation. A more careful approach is necessary before learning and growth can happen.

The **brain stem**, sometimes called the "survival brain" or the "lizard brain," is the most basic part of our brain and is concerned with things like thirst, hunger, and safety. It also governs the body's vital functions such as heart rate, body temperature, and balance. For our purposes here, think of the brain stem as the red light. "Stop!" the Red Brain is saying. "It's not safe to proceed until the light changes."

Remember that the brain stem regulates basic functions related to our survival, so when I say, "not safe to proceed until the light changes," I mean that these basic needs must be satisfied before any higher-level functioning can effectively happen. A common example that most parents would probably recognize is that of a child trying to do homework or practice a musical instrument while hungry or tired. See, the red light is flashing! The child's irritation may be due to some very basic needs, and it is important that you first address those needs before any learning or growth can happen.

The brain is sending signals, like alarms designed to protect us, and it is important not to ignore the signals. The Stoplight Approach to life and parenting helps us recognize the signals our own brains or our children's brains are sending so we can respond appropriately. By using the colors red, yellow, and green for these different signals, parents and children have a simple, everyday language to understand and communicate emotions and needs.

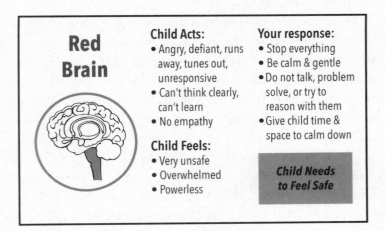

| **Red Brain** | **Child Acts:**
• Angry, defiant, runs away, tunes out, unresponsive
• Can't think clearly, can't learn
• No empathy

Child Feels:
• Very unsafe
• Overwhelmed
• Powerless | **Your response:**
• Stop everything
• Be calm & gentle
• Do not talk, problem solve, or try to reason with them
• Give child time & space to calm down

Child Needs to Feel Safe |

Red Light, Stop!

When Dad is angry, Mom gets tense. When Mom is tense, she starts yelling at the kids, and then the kids start yelling at each other. When we are in Red, people around us tend to go into Red. When we're operating from the brain stem, the survival brain, we sense that things aren't safe for ourselves and for those around us. You might think of this as our brain's warning system telling us, "Danger! Unsafe! Cease normal activity and address the threat."

Red Brain has its place and purpose. For example, it's certainly vital in dangerous situations such as facing a lion in the wild or encountering a thief in the middle of the night. And, of course, we all need the survival brain to govern our basic biological processes. However, scientists have found that living in a constant Red Brain state is unhealthy and can have serious long-term consequences, particularly for children. When someone's brain is always focused on basic needs of survival such as hunger, thirst, and safety, there is often damage that is very difficult to repair, even with the brain's remarkable capacity for healing. According to one study, children who have spent lots of time living in a state of fear or anxiety will experience serious learning and schooling difficulties later on.[2] Spend too much time in your Red Brain, and Green Brain suffers.

Here's another thing about Red Brain: When we're focused on survival and basic needs, we have a reduced capacity for higher-level functions. Scientists have demonstrated that the brain state of a child (or an adult) can have significant influence on his or her thinking and feeling capability.

Dr. Bruce Perry at the Child Trauma Academy has measured the decline of a child's functional IQ while in the different brain states. He's found that when a child is living in a state of fear or extreme anxiety, his or her measurable IQ can drop by as much as half of its full capacity. A child with an IQ of 105 while in a calm, focused state would drop to a range of 55–75 points when a child is feeling fearful or unsafe.[3] So if you are trying to teach your son how to tie his shoes while he's in Red Brain, you might be in for a long ride.

It's not that kids *won't* take in all the information while in Red Brain, it's that they really can't. While your daughter is in Red Brain, working on math homework is not only frustrating, but almost pointless. When children and parents are in Red Brain, they feel unsafe, and their reactions will appear to be irrational and out of control. Indeed, there are really only three ways we react while in Red Brain: fight, flight, or freeze. In other words, we may act angry, run away, or shut down and tune out. It goes without saying that a person in Red Brain has difficulty empathizing with others and can't see another person's perspective.

> Scared children do scary things. . . . Negative behavior does
> not stem from a place of conscious intent, but it stems
> from a place of unconscious fear, unconscious survival.[4]
> DR. B. BRYAN POST

Anyone who has worked with children as a parent or teacher may recognize that the situation that causes a child (or an adult) to shift into Red Brain may not *actually* be dangerous. The survival brain does not always accurately understand whether a threat is real or just perceived. But it's important to remember that, for whatever reason, the person who is truly in a Red Brain state legitimately *feels* unsafe, and we must respond appropriately. If a child is afraid of monsters under the bed, even though we know full well that there are no monsters, we still have to respect genuine feelings of fear, even as we work to show kids that their bed is a safe place.

Children in Red Brain need to feel safe. Once a perceived threat is eliminated or reframed so the child can understand the reality of the situation, the child can then move to Yellow Brain. With appropriate interventions, a Green Brain state can be achieved where successful learning, listening, obeying, and functioning can occur.

Mom is in Yellow Brain!

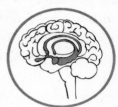

Yellow Brain

Child Acts:
- Irritable
- Unfocused
- Learning takes longer

Child Feels:
- Stressed
- Unsafe
- Unvalued/unloved
- Tired, sick, hungry
- Frustrated
- Shamed

Your Response:
- Look for unmet needs, unsolved problems, lacking skills
- Make them feel safe, valued, & connected

Child Needs to Feel Connected

Yellow Light, Slow Down!

When Mom is stressed, spending time connecting with the kids seems like a distant priority. When Dad is really tired, much of what his wife says may come across as annoying and irrelevant.

Operating from the limbic system, the Yellow Brain state utilizes emotional reactions to address situations. It is important in some circumstances, such as when a mother is advocating for and protecting her children; however, it is not a good state of the brain to be in when consistently making decisions, since logic and facts will have little bearing on responses.

As in Red Brain, there is a reduction of functional IQ in Yellow Brain. In this emotional, feeling state, one's IQ is operating at about only seventy-five percent of full capacity. While learning and growing are possible, these tasks will take longer and require extra effort. When children are in Yellow Brain, they are not as off as in Red Brain mode, but they are still stressed and have unmet needs and unsolved problems. They may be frustrated because they seem to have forgotten certain skills, and as a result of that tension, they feel undervalued.

In the Stoplight Approach, yellow is the warning signal to slow down and assess the situation. Is it safe to proceed slowly? Do we need to slow down because we're going to have to stop soon? Children in Yellow Brain need to feel valued, loved, and connected. Their emotional needs must be satisfied. When someone is able to find ways to fill these emotional needs, the child can return to Green Brain and be more able to learn, listen, and obey.

If your son is whining about being hungry twenty minutes before supper, instead of yelling, tell him that you would be happy to give him a piece of fruit or a vegetable—something that won't spoil his appetite for supper—if he asks politely. This addresses Red Brain's pressing needs and helps him transition back toward Green Brain, without hurting your relationship.

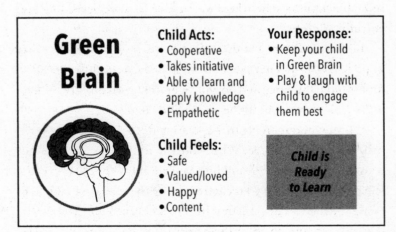

Green Brain

Child Acts:
- Cooperative
- Takes initiative
- Able to learn and apply knowledge
- Empathetic

Child Feels:
- Safe
- Valued/loved
- Happy
- Content

Your Response:
- Keep your child in Green Brain
- Play & laugh with child to engage them best

Child is Ready to Learn

Green Light, Go!

When Dad is happy, he enjoys making pancakes with his kids. When Mom is at peace, reading books with her son becomes a bonding experience. Operating from the neocortex, the Green

Brain state is the highest level of functioning. This should be the default state, and the state we always want to move toward when we find ourselves in Yellow or Red Brain.

Remember, children can have completely different capabilities depending on their current environment and which state their brain is in. When your daughter is operating in the calm, focused Green Brain state, her functional IQ is running at one hundred percent of capacity. This means that she is ready to learn, listen, and obey. It is the best area of the brain for dealing with normal life circumstances.

Green means go! When in Green Brain, we are able to fully engage with our environment, accomplish current tasks, or try new ones. We can also solve problems by integrating new knowledge and applying it to a variety of situations. The brain is in its fullly functioning state where we are able to serve, love, and have empathy for others.

In Green Brain, children do not react to situations; they respond to them. They feel content and stable, and the potential for learning, listening, and obeying is at its maximum. Green Brain is the ideal state for both the parent and child.

It goes without saying that operating from the neocortex is the best state for parents, too. When you're in the Green state and your daughter is fighting with a sibling, you are able to respond in calm, focused ways, helping your children feel safe, loved, and valued. In doing so, you can help them return to a Green Brain state, where they can attempt to solve their own issues and learn from their mistakes. If your teenage son is defying what you've asked him to do, when you're in Green Brain, you can deal with the situation calmly and directly, rather than exasperating him. In Green Brain, just like with a green stoplight signal, we are able to go, responding to situations to the best of our ability.

When you connect to the heart of a child,
everything is possible.[5]

KARYN PURVIS

Be a Brain Detective

Awareness of the state of your child's brain is a big part of learning
how to respond in healthy ways. Sometimes we may assume that
a child is functioning in a Green Brain state when this is not the
case. They may have had little sleep the night before. They may be
under stress because of a bully at school. Or perhaps they're having relationship problems with a friend that we don't know about.
Trying to teach, train, or discipline children while they are in a
Yellow or Red state is counterproductive. In these brain states, they
feel stressed, unsafe, unloved, and undervalued. In order for them
to develop effectively, we must first meet these needs.

A parent's words and actions can create a sense of safety, love,
and value, or a sense of fear, anger, and disrespect. Of course, we
never intend the latter, but it is sometimes too easy to kindle these
feelings in our children if we are unaware of what state our child
is currently in.

Your goal as a parent is to respond to your child in a way that
makes him or her feel emotionally safe and connected to you.
Once you have moved to Green Brain, your child can be coached
to grow new skills and become more resilient. They can learn to
relate to and empathize with others, to decide on their own values,
and engage responsibly with their world.

So consider how you can be a detective. What state is your
child in? What is your child feeling right now? Are they unrespon-
sive or disrespectful, or cooperative and helping others?

Your child may be sending clear signals, but they may also be
bottling up their feelings without any outward expression. Try to

see beyond what you observe on the outside. Consider what unexpressed needs your child may have in the moment. Then respond to your child in a way that makes him feel emotionally safe and connected to you.

Be a Detective

BRAIN STATE	WHAT WE SEE IN CHILD	WHAT WE FEEL	WHAT CHILD FEELS
Red Brain	• Angry • Defiant to instruction • Running away • Tuning out • Completely unresponsive	• Embarrassed • Angry • Fear of failure • Powerless • Desperate	• Very unsafe • Fearful • Overwhelmed • Powerless • Non-empathetic • Stuck
Yellow Brain	• Not focused on task • Irritable • Distracting others • Disrespecting us	• Frustrated • Disrespected • Impatient	• Unsafe • Tired and/or hungry • Sick • Stressed • Frustrated • Shamed
Green Brain	• Focused on a task • Taking initiative • Cooperating • Helping others	• Happy • Proud • Safe • Validated • Respected	• Safe • Happy • Content • Fulfilled • Empathetic

The Most Important Job

We love because he first loved us.

1 JOHN 4:19

When it comes to my teaching, I think I'm pretty good at the job. In fact, my friends tell me I have become somewhat of a perfectionist. But while I have read many parenting books, and I've accumulated all kinds of the right practical experience and knowledge as an educator working with kids, I had to learn that parenting was so much more than I had ever imagined. As a parent, you don't get to go home after a day's work.

Every season of life with each child teaches me new things about myself and my kids. I have sent three of my children off to university, I still have four more children at home, and I have a few foster children as well! Sometimes I face a challenge that makes me feel like I'm parenting for the first time, wrestling with questions that I have never wrestled with before. Technology certainly presents new parenting challenges, with our media and internet-saturated culture pushing all numbers of complex questions into family life. These issues often seem more complicated because of the differing personalities of each of my children, along with the personal choices they are making.

God chose me to parent these children. He doesn't ask me to be a perfect parent, nor does He ask me to parent because I have all the answers. He asks me to be willing. He knows that I won't be able to parent without His help. In my search for hope and for answers, He wants me to find Him.

When I started investigating the principles that make up the Stoplight Approach, I quickly realized that brain science was helping me better understand God's design and His love, and how I need to rely on Him.

Our God is the God of relationship and the God of love. And He seeks an intimate relationship with each of us. There's a reason He so often compares our relationship with Him to that of children and their parents. God is the ultimate caregiver, and as we look to Him, He reveals Himself and how we should parent.

God is the creator of our brain. As we understand more about the brain, more of God is revealed to us. As we know more of God, we are able to understand our children in a different way. As we experience Christ's love, we will be able to grow deeper relationships with our children.

One of the most powerful things I have ever felt was when I looked at a life-size cross with Jesus on it at an old church in England. The statue made Christ feel so tangible in that moment. As I saw the life-sized wounds in the statue's side, my heart had a clear moment of understanding that the Jesus I serve is the Jesus who loves me unconditionally. He has experienced every emotion I have ever felt. Most of all, He understands suffering. He relates to the pain I feel in my heart. During Jesus' time on earth, He felt every emotion I could ever feel—red, yellow, and green.

God knows us better than we do ourselves! With a father's heart, He longs for us to know the safety and love of His presence. He enables us to seek the knowledge that helps us better understand our children, helping them to feel safe and loved. May we learn from Him and live our lives in a way that reflects God's love to our children.

STOPLIGHT REFLECTIONS

1. Can you think of a Red Brain situation that has happened recently in your home? What about a Yellow Brain situation? Green Brain? Brainstorm a few ideas you may have about responding to children who are in the Yellow or Red state while keeping yourself in Green Brain.

2. Reflect on your relationship with God. How does your faith influence your everyday brain states? Are you most often in Red, Yellow, or Green? What does the tone of your voice reveal? What color would you say your own family

members are often in? Does their relationship with God influence their state?

3. Jesus longs for us to experience His love. He wants us to be able to learn and rest in Him. He says, "Come to me, all who labor and are heavy laden, and I will give you rest" (Matthew 11:28). His tender invitation is to satisfy our needs, to move us from the tension and chaos we feel while in "survival" mode and into a state of peacefulness and focus. Picture yourself coming to Him and resting in His arms. Know that He understands you and loves you, that it is in His love that we find a true sense of peace and security.

Prayer

Thank you, God, that we are wondrously made in Your image!
Lord, through Your Holy Spirit, guide me as I learn how our
brains function. Please use this knowledge of Your design to shape
the way I understand, love, and parent my children.

CHAPTER 2

The Heart of Stoplight: Relationship

As I WAS DRIVING, my children started fighting in the back seat of the van. My focus was instantly on their behavior. They are not allowed to fight in the car, and they know this full well. I told them to stop, but they continued. I was growing angry, feeling a loss of control and a disrespect of my authority, so the volume in my voice increased. Next, I was yelling at them to stop the bickering. "If you don't stop immediately, everyone is going to their room when we get home!" I shouted over my shoulder.

I suppose most parents have had similar experiences, times when you feel disrespected and that your only effective parenting tactic is to simply overwhelm your kids with volume and authority. But as I learn more and more about what makes my kids tick, I start to pause more often to analyze what is really going on. As mentioned earlier, recognizing the current situation and what

Stoplight state my kids are in is a crucial part of the Stoplight Approach to parenting.

In this situation, it didn't take long to determine what was going on. It was the end of a long day. My kids were feeling stressed. They were tired and hungry, and they needed some space to unwind. It seemed they were operating more in the Yellow Brain state, and I recognized that their ability to handle stress was limited. So when one child dumped a backpack on top of someone else's stuff or started reading a book that another sibling wanted to read first, a fight broke out. Of course, I wasn't helping matters any by adding my volume to the mix.

I needed to recognize what was really happening and address my children and their needs instead of their behavior. There are a few ways I've learned that can change my approach when my kids are fighting in the car.

1. I can prepare some snacks ahead of time (or stop and buy some) if it is still a long trip home. As any parent of young kids understands, a fun snack instantly changes the whole dynamic in the car, satisfying a Red Brain need and helping move kids into Green.

2. I redirect the focus of the ride home, starting a positive discussion about their day: "What was your favorite part of today?" I know that if I bring myself back to Green, I can often get the kids in Green.

3. I can stop the car, validate their feelings by recognizing that they are tired and hungry, and reassure them that soon we will be home and they can have a snack. I can calmly explain how it is unsafe for me to drive the car if they are fighting, as it distracts me, and ask them if we can find a solution together so we can get home safely.

Later, when the kids are in Green, we can plan for tomorrow on how we are going to act at our best in the car. There are times I have taken my kids back to the car while in Green, having them practice going in and out of the car in a way that feels safe for everyone. I am not being permissive and letting my children fight. Instead, I am finding a way that I can train them so they can learn to the best of their abilities.

A Change of Focus

It happens to many parents: When a child disobeys, parents react. Parents have a choice in how they respond to a child's misbehavior. They can react in anger and annoyance, or they can respond calmly with patience and love. All over the world, parents and caregivers use the approach they know best to deal with their children when they disobey. Do we focus on the child or the child's behavior? Do we focus on past actions or future skills?

Many parents grew up learning about parenting by watching their own parents' strategy of focusing on a child's behavior, both current and past. One common approach is employing punishment in response to a child's disobedience, hoping the child will remember the consequences they have endured and therefore make better decisions in the future. While careful implementation of consequences for a child's misbehavior is a part of wise parenting, an ongoing focus on punishment for bad choices can leave kids living in fear.

The Stoplight Approach is less fear-based and more relationship-based parenting, keeping the focus on the child and the relationship with the child, while still training them so that they can gain the skills they need to act appropriately in the future.

This is like God's approach with us. He sees us as children who are broken and in need of healing. He says, "I am your safety. I am your refuge." He knows that we need to feel safe before He can train us. He says, "I love you!" even as He recognizes us for who we truly are—sinners in need of a Savior. He takes us in our mess and makes us feel safe and loved, and in the context of that relationship, He grows us.

The Heat of the Moment

The empty biscuit package lay on the floor, tell-tale evidence that one of the kids had discovered the special treat I was saving for Christmas day. I was frustrated and very angry, so we decided it would be better for my husband to handle this incident.

Later that evening, the culprit asked me if I would watch a movie with her. Despite my years of being a Stoplight parent, my first thought was *No! You disrespected me and violated my privacy, you've ruined a Christmas surprise for your siblings, and you definitely don't deserve to have a pleasant, cozy evening with me.*

Thankfully, I stopped and took a deep breath before answering. I remembered some parenting lessons I had just been studying, summed up by Dr. Jane Nelsen, a family therapist and author of the Positive Discipline series of books: "Where did we get the crazy idea that in order to make children do better, we first have to make them feel worse?"[1]

What would refusing her request accomplish? She might feel disconnected and sad, not because of her actions, but because I wasn't taking time to be with her. She might feel unloved and unsafe, downgrading into Red Brain for the rest of the evening. So I sat down and watched the movie with her. There were still consequences to her actions that we had to work through, but by maintaining a tangible connection with me, she was in the right brain state to learn and grow.

When our children misbehave, it is natural to feel hurt as a parent, especially over issues that feel like a personal attack. (I really wanted that package of cookies!) When we focus on that hurt, we can justify what amounts to revenge by framing it as a consequence of the behavior. We need to stop and assess whether what we are doing is teaching the child a valuable skill or merely making ourselves feel better because now our child is hurting as much as we are hurting.

Love Versus Fear

Many parents have probably heard that it is possible to spoil a child by loving him or her too much. Kids need a little toughness here and there, we are told, to prepare them for the real world. Sure, a certain amount of tough love is needed sometimes, but no legitimate parenting strategy removes love from the relationship, even if your kids don't immediately recognize that your actions are loving and are meant for their good.

So, no, you can't love your kids too much. And science has demonstrated that, in responding to kids' behaviors and even misbehaviors, loving responses—as opposed to responses that rely on fear of punishment—actually increase their capacity to grow, learn, and develop. Given what we've learned about the different states of the human brain, this makes sense. A child who is in a state of fear is operating more from the limbic system and the brain stem. Remember that Yellow or Red Brain can lower functional IQ by as much as half. This just isn't a good place for a child to be when parents want to help a child learn to make good decisions. Getting back to Green is mission one.

"Brain science is showing that when children are in a state of fear, they are not operating out of their rational brains, the neocortex. Instead, they are operating from the limbic system, the emotional brain," writes Heather Forbes, founder of the Beyond Consequences parenting organization. "Their decisions reflect their emotional state. . . . Their interpretation of what you say to them will not be processed from a logical, sequential, or reasonable perspective. It will be processed from a perspective of fear and negativity."[2]

Fear hinders learning, while love enables learning. Love reveals value and provides safety. Love must be the basis of our relationships, and providing that sense of security and safety is our primary concern when dealing with misbehavior.

> There is no fear in love, but perfect love casts out fear. For fear has to do with punishment, and whoever fears has not been perfected in love.
>
> 1 JOHN 4:18

The Stoplight Approach might sound foreign if you've been raised to recognize a more fear-based style of parenting, but it is

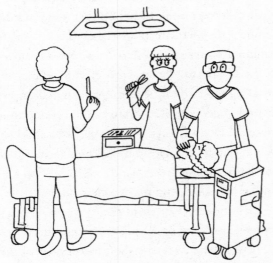

"I can't remember how to perform knee surgery on someone from New York; I can only remember the procedure for people from South Africa!"

easier than you might think to implement. It requires patience and perseverance, but the outcome is rewarding and life-giving. And it works for every kind of family.

Whether it is knee surgery, a broken arm, or a case of malaria, a person's culture does not determine how they should be medically treated. The human body is the human body. It is the same with brain science. Regardless of race, culture, people group, education, or background, we are all human beings designed by God to experience similar reactions to perceived danger or the sense of being unloved or undervalued. When exposed to a threat, adrenaline surges, blood flow increases, and a host of other physiological changes occur—including changes in our brain.

Emotional Self-Control

To be an effective parent, physical and emotional safety for both ourselves and our children is crucial. As parents we must do as much as we can to understand what our kids' brains are saying so that we can help them be safe and feel safe.

And children need to understand the signals their own brain is sending them. The Stoplight Approach is an effective, easy-to-grasp metaphor for children. If I am out running errands, I can call home and ask my young kids what color they are in because they understand the stoplight colors and what they mean. My youngest child might say, "Green! I'm playing with the puppies!" My eleven-year-old, on the other hand, might say, "Yellow, but I've started reading my book, so I'm almost back to Green."

Children's awareness of their own emotional state and their ability to take actions to "get back to Green" are a big part of developing emotional intelligence. Scientists have also shown that emotional intelligence (usually referred to as EQ) is a better predictor than IQ for success in the workplace, as well as overall happiness and life satisfaction. Psychologist Daniel Goleman, author of the ground-breaking book *Emotional Intelligence*, estimates that cognitive skills make up only around 20 percent of the factors that determine success in life, with EQ making up a much larger share of the determining factors. (Other factors include temperament, family education, wealth, and plain old luck.) Since Goleman's work, several other studies have continued to demonstrate the importance of emotional intelligence, showing that it is a better predictor of future success in school, careers, health, relationships, and overall quality of life.[3]

The Stoplight Approach emphasizes healthy emotional self-control. The key components of EQ are Awareness (emotional literacy), Behavior (self-regulation), Connection (empathy), Decision (moral identity), Engagement (social responsibility) and Frequency (growth mindset). We often call these key areas the Stoplight ABCs, and we'll discuss them in greater detail in later chapters.

> Fire can warm or consume,
> water can quench or drown,
> wind can caress or cut.
> And so it is with human relationships:
> we can both create and destroy,
> nurture and terrorize, traumatize
> and heal each other.[4]

BRUCE PERRY & MAIA SZALAVITZ

Beloved Children of God

> I praise you, for I am fearfully and wonderfully
> made. Wonderful are your works; my soul knows it
> very well.

PSALM 139:14

Have you ever wondered what God thinks when He looks at your life? What does He think when we mess up? What lens does He see us through?

I believe that God doesn't look at our lives with disappointment—seeing us as "bad children"—but with a certain amount of loving sadness because we keep making the same mistakes over and over again. When God looks at me, He sees a child whom He loves, even in my brokenness. He loves me in spite of that brokenness. Yet He wants me to grow in my understanding of His love and His truth so that I might better reflect His image to the world.

Neither does God want to punish any of us for the things we've done wrong, sending us to our rooms for a time out until we're ready to listen. That doesn't reflect our God's character. He is always ready to listen. We can always turn toward His love. He wants to speak to your heart. *Come to Me. Bring Me your anger. Bring Me your mess. I'm big enough. And I will give you rest. I am your fortress, and I will protect you.*

God delights in us! "The LORD . . . will rejoice over you with gladness; he will quiet you by his love; he will exult over you with loud singing" (Zephaniah 3:17). He rejoices over us, for we are His beloved children. It is God's character to love and have mercy, bringing us back into relationship with Him.

When I first started looking at the science and Scripture that now shape the Stoplight Approach, I realized that I needed to better understand the God who designed us. And by better understanding the creation, I am learning to see myself through the Creator's eyes. *I am fearfully and wonderfully made.* This is my mantra, which I remind myself to say even when I don't believe it.

Despite my mistakes, God still delights in me. And while His love is unconditional, He doesn't leave us in our mess. He wants to teach us, to help us grow as He draws us into a relationship with Him.

STOPLIGHT REFLECTIONS

1. How do you feel in a situation where raised voices, threats, and shame are used? With that response in mind, how do you feel in a situation where you are heard, understood, and helped? Now, which is your more instinctive reaction to a child's misbehavior?

2. Think back to a time you focused on past misbehavior instead of future skills. What could you have done differently in that situation? What small steps can you take to change your parenting to a Stoplight Approach?

3. Consider how you think God looks at you. How does God's character resemble the Stoplight Approach? In what areas of your life is God training you?

─────────────── *Prayer* ───────────────

I adore You, God, for You have made me in Your love and *for* Your love! No matter how many times I mess up, You are always waiting for me to turn back to You. Help me rest in Your love and forgiveness each day. Fill me with Your loving presence that I may reflect Your tender care to my children.

CHAPTER 3

Our Heart, Their Brain: Attachment

WHEN CATHERINE WAS BORN and I held my oldest daughter for the first time, I loved her immediately. I brought her to my breast, cradling this tiny infant as she nuzzled closer. In the months that followed, her spontaneous smiles and happy gurgles at my presence made all the interrupted nights, frequent feedings, and changed diapers a constant joy. Catherine was a securely attached child.

My husband and I adopted Beth. When I held my daughter for the first time, I loved her immediately. I brought her to my heart, hugging this tiny toddler as she smiled at me the way she did at any kind stranger. In the months that followed, her spontaneous temper-tantrums and piercing screams of "I hate you" made all the interrupted nights, frequent demands, and parental caring a constant struggle. Beth was an unattached child.

I've always wanted my children to be able to rest with me. To just be in our home and feel safe and secure in our presence.

But I noticed a difference between my biological children and my adopted children. At the end of a busy day, my biological children would always want to rest with me, to cuddle with me. But my adopted daughter was never really comfortable with this sort of affection. She did not want to cuddle with me. She would flip her body away from me, trying to push me away. I pleaded with and cried to God—I wanted my little girl to sense my love. I wanted her to feel loved and secure when she was with me. But maybe it wasn't what she needed. I had to recognize an uncomfortable fact, that *I* wanted her to want my love. *For me.* And I was starting to feel . . . *used.* For example, she had no problem coming to me for a cookie or something else she wanted.

As I wrestled with this, I sensed God speaking to me. This doesn't happen often in my life, but the message was clear: *You're just like her.* Do I only turn to God when I need something? Or do I ever simply rest with Him?

The Heart of Attachment

When our son Peter cries, my husband or I comfort him. When our daughter Jessica is sick, we tend to her needs. When Rachel is afraid of the dark, we snuggle her. We are creating attachments with our children.

As we discussed earlier, relationships are critical to our emotional well-being. Central to our ability to form healthy relationships is whether we experienced necessary attachment with our parents in the first years of our lives. Attachment is the process where an infant or child discovers that their physical and emotional needs will be met by their parent or caregiver. Diane Benoit, a professor of psychiatry at the University of Toronto, writes that attachment is particularly crucial and brain-changing when a child is "hurt, sick, or afraid."[1]

Attachment issues as a child can affect relationships long into the adult years. Parenting style, economic status, or an organized home life—these things do not define the healthy development of a child nearly as much as attachment does.

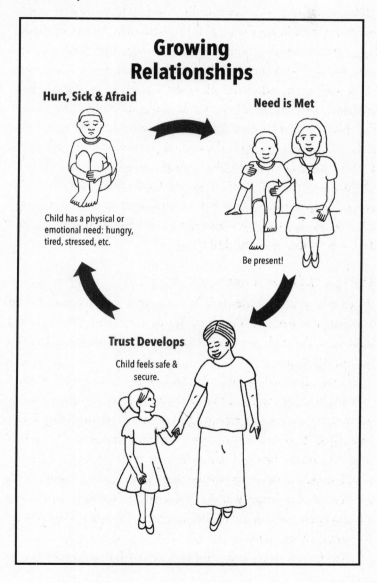

When you are asked to list an emergency contact, who do you put? Likely it is someone close to you whom you love and trust during those difficult times in life. Those who don't have emergency contacts are likely going to have a harder time when faced with a crisis.

Think of attachment as a child's emergency contact information. A well-attached child who is hurt, sick, or afraid will turn to the person they are attached to for help. When we are there for them in those hard times, we increase their resilience and their ability to face the world. At these times, your relationship with your child has the most potential for growth. We'll look at the topic of resilience more in the next chapter.

The process of attachment with children strongly depends on healthy relationships between the adults in the home. If there is constant conflict in a home, the attachment process can be hindered, because parents are short on the emotional capacity to properly care for and bond with their child.

If your relationships are strong, the foundation of attachment for your children will be strong. In my marriage, Thursdays are date days. My husband and I set aside the afternoon to do something as a couple while our children are at school. Every few months, we also try to go away for a night or two to reconnect and deepen our relationship. Intentional commitment to dates is a lot cheaper than marriage counseling or divorce fees!

Philip Mamalakis, author of *Parenting Toward the Kingdom*, recognizes the deep significance of a child's attachment to his or her parents:

> Children behave better when they feel connected to us. Why is it that our children demand our attention just when we are busiest, before company arrives, or when we are in a hurry to leave? It's because in those moments they feel disconnected from us. We need to prioritize

connecting with our children daily and teaching them how to seek connection in constructive ways by using their words, asking to talk, asking for time or a hug, and learning how to share what might be troubling them.[2]

An Attachment Comparison

Baby Grace lives in a simple hut just a few steps from a busy road. She has rags for clothes and has never had the luxury of using a diaper. Grace's mother has her daughter secured to her back in the traditional African way while working hard at preparing food three times a day every day of the week. A sense of safety and connection is displayed between Baby Grace and her mother such that Grace cries when Mom is not there and instantly smiles when she returns. Grace may never go to school or own a pretty dress, but she will grow up knowing how to have healthy relationships with her peers, her future husband, and her future children.

Luke grew up with everything money could buy. He had a father with a great-paying job. He had nannies to care for him and drivers to take him everywhere he wanted to go.

In the first few days after Luke was born, his mother began leaving him with his grandmother, and Luke's father was consistently absent because of his dedication to work.

This left Luke with limited opportunities to attach and feel safe with his parents. Throughout his life, Luke had the best education possible, but as he grew older, he began looking for acceptance and connection anywhere he could find it. His need for connection was so strong that he was willing to do anything to gain it. He got involved in drugs, alcohol, violent crimes, and developed aggressive behavior. Without intentional attachment intervention, where he would be taught how to connect to a caregiver, Luke would most likely not be able to have strong, healthy relationships with those around him. Getting and keeping a job, getting married, and nurturing children would be more difficult for him.

The attachment relationship is an important process that starts in a newborn baby and develops between an infant and his or her caregiver. It directly contributes to the child's emotional and problem-solving areas of the brain. Attachment is crucial to social development.

"I know you need me."

A child should have a primary caregiver, someone he intuitively goes to above everyone else. Most children have a secondary caregiver, who they also feel safe with and loved by unconditionally, but the relationship is not as intimate as with the primary caregiver.

If a child has many different primary caregivers over the first two years of life, he or she is less likely to become attached to anyone. As mentioned above, this can be seriously detrimental to a person's ability to develop healthy relationships. This is why being intentional with your attachment is crucial.

When your child is hurt, sick, or afraid, they will signal their need for attention. Whether through crying, reaching, crawling, or speaking, the child is requesting the caregiver's immediate response. And this becomes a healthy cycle that builds attachment. When you respond to their needs, their stress is reduced. The child learns to trust that their needs will be met, that their world is safe, and he or she is now able to explore and be curious in their environment, leading to healthy brain development.

In Stoplight language, when babies and young children are hurt, sick, or afraid, they are generally in Yellow or Red Brain. A caregiver meeting their needs helps them back to Green Brain. As this process is repeated over and over again, strong, healthy connections to and within the neocortex are developed.

How you respond to the child can also determine the type and quality of attachment. This attachment type impacts the rest of that child's life. When needs have been met promptly and consistently, the brain builds healthy Green connections, so that, as children mature, they are able to switch to and keep themselves in the Green Brain state more easily. Baby Grace, from the sidebar above, has the relational resources needed to be a productive member of society, due to years of positive responses given by her mother. Luke's lack of responses and inconsistency from a primary caregiver when he was a young child resulted in a more difficult life for him as an adult, and he may grow up to be a detriment to society if there is no intervention.

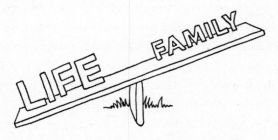

The busyness of life often weighs heavier than our family, but we must prioritize healthy relationships and attachments.

Time Together

After my husband and I adopted our three youngest children, we took a family road trip across Canada. The older kids sat with the younger kids, reading stories, playing games, singing songs, building attachment. The seating arrangement changed every day, so everyone had a different older sibling for each ride. We stopped at hundreds of parks, historical sites, churches, gas stations, and friends' homes over the trip, building memories wherever we went. Some people might see the idea of nine people, including seven children, driving across the country as absolutely crazy. It wasn't about the scenery for our family, though. It was about creating healthy attachments with our newly adopted children, giving them the safety of having their new family close all the time.

Time as a family is crucial for attachment. You might not drive across a country, but you could set aside evenings or a day every week to spend time as a family. Go hiking, make a meal, play board games, write cards to each other; make sure there is a balance between family time and the rest of life's business to create safe attachments with your kids.

When you play with your child, follow their interests, and allow them to choose activities. This gives them a sense of ownership and control during playtime. You will then find that your child will become more cooperative in other moments.

Becoming a Forever Family

At age fifteen, my eldest daughter gave this advice to parents who were bringing children into the family:

Know that all children will test you, especially adopted siblings. Often, they'll say things like, "I hate you." It's only because they want to know if their family's love is permanent. Show the kids you love them no matter what. My mom hugs my sister until she calms down while telling her she'll always be her mommy.

When a new child enters the home, make sure siblings have the chance to learn and know about each other. Children in a family should learn to be friends with each other. My mom says friends will come and go, but your siblings will always be your family.

Set aside family time. We have family meals at a big table where we talk about our day. Things like family outings are important for bonding as a family, as well. It's all about unity. Everyone is not a separate little piece; we're part of a big family.

One-on-One Time

The 5-10-5 rule is a vital way to build the parent-child relationship. When a child first wakes up in the morning, they need five minutes of one-on-one time with a parent to reconnect after a long night. After school, the child needs at least ten minutes to spend with their parent reconnecting in one-on-one time. The day finishes out with five minutes before bed. While more time is always great, of course, being intentional about these small blocks of time will help you build a healthy relationship with your child. This can be easier said than done, especially with a larger family—and of course it requires you to intentionally carve out time in your schedule, but these positive moments at regular intervals are an essential part of helping your child build and maintain attachment to you.

Sitting around the supper table as a family, while very important, doesn't count as part of the 5-10-5 minutes. This time needs to be one-on-one, and it should not involve talking about misbehavior or other ongoing issues. It is time to focus on the child— their thoughts, ideas, interests, and dreams. The activities of this time will be different with each child, whether that is a walk, a snuggle, a story, or just a conversation over tea. Wherever and whenever you create these minutes of connection, you as the parent must be fully emotionally present. Put the phone away! This is an investment. The long-term benefits to your child and your relationship make it more than worth it.

Following a challenging time in my life, our family ended up living with a priest in England. The priest challenged me on the value of liturgy and connecting with God first thing in the morning, in the afternoon, and at the end of the day. I began to realize that the 5-10-5 rule aligns with what Christians have done for thousands of years with their morning, afternoon, and night prayers. We need to be intentional with our relationships throughout the day—with our children just as we are with God. No relationship can grow unless you are intentional about nurturing it.

If you find that you are dealing with more challenging behaviors in your child, you may need to spend more time with them. Challenging behaviors come out of disconnection.

Dr. B. Bryan Post recommends that parents double the

connection time to 10-20-10 for children who are particularly challenging. He calls this the Attachment Prescription.[3]

Building Attachment with a Challenging Child

I don't really know where my liver is, but I can assure you that if it suddenly stopped working, I would learn all about it. I would become very aware of how it functions and how I could keep it healthy in the future. There's nothing like a serious problem to make us sit up and pay attention.

I think the same is true with an unattached child. Attachment with biological children often happens intuitively. With children who haven't learned attachment in the first two years of life, parents are keenly aware of their need to constantly pursue the child, even when they push us away. It requires intentional effort and a long-term focus. They understand that if this child makes no attachments, the outcome will be devastating.

Attachment is about creating new templates in the child's brain. Children without parental figures in their first year of life have been found to have high levels of cortisol, which is produced in response to stress hormones and serves as a measure of stress. Their brains are on high alert, meaning the child is forced to learn and grow while living in Red Brain. And as we saw earlier, living in a constant state of Red Brain can have negative repercussions for a child's future in school, work, and relationships. We are not meant to always be focused on survival. We are not meant to live in fear and stress.

Each one of my children who were adopted transitioned into our home differently depending on their background. As their parent, it was always my priority to create safe attachment with each of them. One child needed to be taught how to express pain. At two years old, she fell down our stairs, but she didn't cry. In her early years, no one had nurtured her when she was hurt, sick, or afraid. It was as if she'd actually lost her voice, like she no longer believed anyone was noticing her. We had to be intentional with caring for these needs as soon as we saw them surface.

Another child wouldn't let us pick him up or hold him as a baby. The only way my husband could get him to sit on his lap was if he enticed him with his cellphone. I would get up in the middle of the night just to hold and rock him while he was in a deep sleep, to create some attachment. As time went on, I would go in to hold him earlier and earlier in the night, when he wasn't so deeply asleep. It was a long process, but eventually he started coming to us on his own.

Still another child wanted to drink from a baby bottle when she came to us, even though she was much too old for one. We allowed her to drink from it while she sat on our lap. The bottle was a distraction; the real goal was helping her become comfortable sitting with us.

My husband and I were intentional, especially in those first few years, about finding activities that required touch between our children and us: swimming, foot rubs, fun wrestling games, etc. And I was keenly aware of my kids' need to connect with their parents. During the first six months, I didn't leave my adopted children with anyone. Often times, friends would offer to hold my children at church, but I would say no. It was not because I didn't trust my friends, but because my children were still learning how to attach to me as their mother.

Though a lot of our methods went against what most parents would consider age-appropriate, our children had missed important developmental stages. We were going back in an effort to recreate the attachment that had been missed. Now, years later, our attachment with these kids is much stronger. It is something we still have to work on intentionally, but they now know we are their caregivers, and they readily come to us when they are hurt, sick, or afraid.

Hurt People Hurt People

The brain develops differently in a child without attachment to a primary caregiver than it does in a child with a secure attachment. In fact, these kids are affected at the very core of how they understand the world. As unattached kids grow and someone shows love to them, they are unable to easily accept that love, and will often outright reject affection.

Many of the issues in our society are actually rooted in insecure attachments. The potential for inappropriate relationships and failures in marriages, parenting, and jobs increases significantly in insecurely attached adults. These relationships are characterized by mistrust, anger, and anxiety. Often, they can neither share their feelings nor believe that they are lovable.

Insecure attachment can also go so far as to lead to mental illnesses such as psychopathic behaviors, violence, oppositional defiant disorder (ODD), conduct disorder (CD), depression, and even post-traumatic stress disorder (PTSD) in some children, especially if there is no intervention. In the Stoplight understanding, these conditions are what we would classify as Red Attachment because these children perceive their world as hostile. They may appear to have unpredictable friendliness or may not exhibit emotions appropriately. These children find it difficult to receive signals of love, appreciation, and care. They are often unable to handle their emotions.

Secure attachment must be what you give a child who has gone through traumatic experiences. This must happen before any trauma work can be accomplished, and it can only come through safe, secure relationships.

Creating attachment with your unattached child is not impossible. But because they have missed certain developmental stages in their early years, it will not happen automatically or intuitively. Be intentional about connection. Create a family environment of trust-based relationships for your child to grow and become safe in. It takes hard work and a lot of time, but always remember that there is hope. Your ongoing love and pursuit of your children can truly change the course of their lives.

Creating Attachment with Children Who Missed Out

Go back developmentally. Your child has missed crucial points in their development that need to be re-created.

Keep the child close. Just as you would a newborn baby, spend time with your child and don't send them off to programs that you believe make your life easier.

Look for nurturing moments. Intentionally and proactively look for moments when your child is hurt, sick, or afraid, and go to them. Do not wait for them to seek you out.

An Active Pursuit. Reinforce your role as caregiver to your child through playing games such as Hide-n-Seek. Reassure them that even though they were lost, you are actively seeking them out.

Physical touch. Intentionally play activities that encourage gentle physical touch such as swimming, basketball, or play wrestling.

Physical needs. Reassure your child that you are providing for their physical needs. Help them understand that food, water, and shelter will always be available.

What Helps My Child's Brain?

Dr. Daniel Siegel's research has shown that when an infant and their parent are engaged, even without the use of words, crucial areas of the infant's prefrontal cortex are developing and becoming organized. In his book *The Whole-Brain Child*, Siegel says these developing functions include regulation, social cognition, empathy, response flexibility, self-awareness, and fear modulation.[4]

In Stoplight language, these healthy brain skills are what we

mean when we mention Green Brain development. And, again, such developments don't occur when the infant spends a lot of time alone. When humans are forming a secure attachment, there are thousands of successful interactions with a caregiver, plus a small number of unsuccessful—but not devastating—ones.

As they grow, securely attached children start recognizing that they are safe. These are children who can investigate the environment away from their parents, who are a secure base from which to explore and build friendships. They are able to do this because they know they are loved and cared for when they have needs. Children who have secure attachments are also more resilient because they believe that they are lovable, that trusting their parents is wise, and that others will help them when they have needs. These children recognize that parents help them to get snuggles, explore the world, calm down, solve problems, and reduce pain.

By school age, a secure child is able to create and maintain friendships and knows how to give up some of their wants for the sake of others. This pattern of self-sacrifice prepares them for healthy friendships, marriage, and parenthood later in life.

The Power in Healthy Touch

From the moment of birth, our kids need to be physically loved and cared for. Dr. Siegel reminds us that most nurturing takes place nonverbally. Parents have the power to communicate so much without even speaking:

> The most powerful nonverbal response of all is one that you probably do automatically: you touch your child. You put your hand on her arm. You pull her close to you. You rub her back. You hold her hand. A loving touch—whether subtle, like the squeeze of a hand, or more demonstrative, like a full, warm embrace—has the power to quickly defuse a heated situation. The reason is that when we feel someone touch us in a way that's nurturing and loving, feel-good hormones (like oxytocin) are released into our brain and body, and our levels of cortisol, a stress hormone, decrease. In other words, giving your kids loving physical affection literally and beneficially alters their brain chemistry.[5]

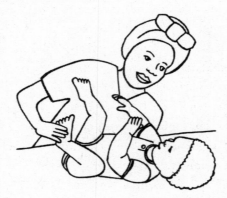

Most parents have observed one remarkable benefit of a healthy physical connection: When a child is feeling upset, a loving touch can really help calm things down and help you two connect. Touch is one powerful way we communicate with our children nonverbally.

Connecting Whole or Half-Heartedly

I heard a knocking at my bedroom door. I rolled over to check the time: two o'clock a.m. The knocking continued, followed by the door opening slowly. "Mom?" Rachel stood at the side of my bed, crying, "I had a bad dream."

Most parents probably agree that connecting with your child is the last thing you want to do when you've just been pulled away from a deep slumber at two in the morning. But parenting is a full-time job, and being intentional about connecting with your child during their time of distress will have long-term benefits for their brain development, as well as deepening your relationship.

When we looked at the examples of Luke and Grace, we saw what was ultimately required for the development of each child—connection with the parent. A Stoplight parent values this ongoing connection, saying, "I want my child to stay in Green and have a safe environment, and this may mean sacrificing an activity (and maybe some sleep) so that I can have time with them."

My house tends to get very crazy with all the kids and all their individual needs. Sometimes it can be too easy to overlook a child. To avoid this, we practice Mommy time and Daddy time in which each of our children is able to do something they enjoy with our undivided attention for a specific amount of time. This could be just the two of us going to the grocery store for ice cream, taking a work trip with Mom for two weeks, or spending the weekend joining in with Dad's plans. Mommy time and Daddy time are things they look forward to and have the ability to ask us for, which gives them a sense of belonging, knowing that they are deserving of our time and attention.

Their Lives Outside Home

Connection goes beyond your interactions at home and the relationship you have with each of your children. Real connection also includes an involvement in their lives and interests, and especially an awareness of their relationships with other people. Do you *really* know your children? How involved are you in their life outside your home? Do you know their friends?

It is, of course, important for our children to have friends. But this is an area of their lives that requires great interest of parents. As Dr. Gordon Neufeld has explored in his book *Hold on to Your Kids: Why Parents Need to Matter More Than Peers*, a child's relationship with peers, and their valuing peers over parents, can cause some big issues in family relationships, especially with younger children. When children spend excessive time with peers rather than parents, they begin to lose their sense of direction and even begin to transfer some of their dependence from their parents to their friends.[6]

Building relationships between families is a healthier way of creating a community and providing your children with positive peers. This means your children have friends and other adults building into their lives. And, in a way, it is a means of creating extended family, even if we don't have biological family nearby. Safe adults can build attachments with your children, and they pour positive influence into their lives on top of your own parental guidance. My children have many aunties and uncles who are not biologically related to us, but relationships give them the connections and closeness of family members. The adults in our community are interesting and welcoming people that bring security and diversity to all my children.

It's important to note that many children will interact differently with their various friends. Some friends will bring out the silly side of your child, the violent side, the playful side, or the quiet side. It's important to be aware of this, so that you know what to expect and how to address it in advance. Sometimes your child may need a break from certain friends or have a shorter time for their play date.

Relationship Is Everything

As a parent, you cannot "spoil" a child with too much emotional connection. Large quantities of time, attention, and love are never the reason a child is spoiled. Spoiling is permissiveness, giving children what they want simply because they said so. It gives them a sense of entitlement, an "I get what I want, when I want it, how I want it" sort of mindset. Needless to say, this is not an authentic connection with your child.

Being a Stoplight parent means training in the context of relationship. It means ensuring that your children feel emotionally safe before dealing with behavioral issues. Relationship always precedes behavior.

"I love my children, but I don't I think I like them very much." Have your ever thought this or admitted this aloud before? I totally understand this tension. My own prayer is that I delight in my children even when they haven't earned it. Even when they absolutely have not been lovable!

It's easy to delight in my son when his chores and homework are all done, and he wants to sit with me and chat. It's easy to delight in my daughter when she's just finished the dishes without being told. But then . . . I walk into her room in the morning to wake her up, and all I see is an incredible mess, tangled hair, and mismatched clothes. When I'm in Yellow Brain—overwhelmed, stressed, and running late—instead of greeting my children with love and delight in the morning, I often greet them with a sense of disappointment and a critical spirit. When I start the day with a negative tone, I lose sight of the beautiful children God has given me! And when I focus on the one area they may have failed in, do they feel loved?

One of the most shocking things I realized as I learned about brain science was that it is impossible to make a child feel loved when the parent is in Yellow or Red. They feel our stress! They feel our disapproval!

As I grew up, I realized that this was also mirrored in my perceptions of God. I had this idea that there was a Jesus who was always disappointed in me.

In other words, while I never questioned God's love for me, I still didn't feel that God liked me very much. Like a parent can make a child feel, I didn't feel like I was ever good enough.

If I want my children to not just have a knowledge of love, but to *feel* loved, I need to delight in them no matter what the circumstances—even despite their rudeness or misbehavior. Why? Because God loves *me* despite my sin. Even in my mess-ups! I don't have to earn His love. I need to pursue my children and show an interest in them, just as God pursues a relationship with me.

The Connection of Our Father

When I thought, "My foot slips,"
>your steadfast love, O LORD, held me up.
When the cares of my heart are many,
>your consolations cheer my soul.

PSALM 94:18-19

God, our perfect Father, seeks to build connection and attachment with His children. Throughout Scripture, we see example after example of God being with us when we are hurt, sick, and afraid. He is with us when we cannot sense His presence, whether we are in a state of Red, Yellow, or Green.

In the life of Jesus, we see most clearly who God really is:

tenderly healing the sick and injured, comforting those who are afraid, giving dignity to those who are despised, and inviting all to come into a genuine relationship with God. Jesus helps us build our attachment with God, our Father.

However, Jesus' ministry on earth was twofold: He did not come simply to preach, or only to heal—He did both. As parents, we also need to make sure we do not neglect one or the other. We need to be with our children: comforting them in times of trouble, bandaging their scrapes, and taking them to the doctor when they need to be healed. But it is also our job to teach and to guide our children, to ensure they are learning the skills they will need in order to be successful adults. In fact, helping our children when they are hurt, sick, and afraid, teaches them how to have healthy relationships.

God seeks attachment with us. When Jesus finished His earthly ministry, He made us a promise that the Holy Spirit would be with us. Also named Helper and Comforter, the Holy Spirit is God's promise to be there when we are hurt, sick, or afraid.

Let us seek to build attachment with our children by teaching them, caring for them, and spending time with them, both when they are doing well and when they are struggling.

How God Models Attachment
Read the following verses from Scripture and consider what they teach us about our Heavenly Father. How does God model attachment to us as His adopted children? How can you model these same principles to your children?

God Pursues Us
"For the Son of Man came to seek and to save the lost" (Luke 19:10).

God didn't wait until we were "good." He showed His love for us by seeking us while we were still lost. So, too, we don't wait for our children to be good before we pour out our love. We seek them out. We pour love into their lives. We seek to establish attachment while they are still lost in anger, guilt, and fear.

God Relates Uniquely to Us

"But as it is, God arranged the members in the body, each one of them, as he chose" (1 Corinthians 12:18).

God relates to us in our uniqueness. He doesn't treat us all the same. He embraces our differences and uses us in His Kingdom as individuals. Each child in our care is unique and will require a different approach to care and discipline, and different demonstrations of love.

God's Love Is Intentional

"He chose us in him before the foundation of the world, that we should be holy and blameless before him" (Ephesians 1:4).

God is intentional in His love for you. He had a plan from the creation of the world that you would be part of His family. We need to be intentional about our attachment and love toward our children. We need to decide how and when we will show love to each child each day. We must be intentional about our kids' need for attachment.

God Provides Safety

"The name of the Lord is a strong tower; the righteous man runs into it and is safe" (Proverbs 18:10).

Before you can have attachment, you must feel safe. God promises to be our refuge, a safe place in which there is no fear. Likewise, we need to provide a safe environment, both physically and emotionally, for our children. Until a child feels safe, they will not trust. Until they can trust, they will not attach. Until they attach, they will not love.

God Delights in Us

"The LORD your God is in your midst, a mighty one who will save; he will rejoice over you with gladness; he will quiet you by his love; he will exult over you with loud singing" (Zephaniah 3:17).

God takes great pleasure and delight in us. He takes great joy in us turning to and being with Him. We need to take joy in being with our children. We need to delight in who they are and in the sheer pleasure of being able to share life with them.

God Is Responsive and Gentle

"Come to me, all who labor and are heavy laden, and I will give you rest. Take my yoke upon you, and learn from me, for I am gentle and lowly in heart, and you will find rest for your souls. For my yoke is easy, and my burden is light" (Matthew 11:28-30).

Jesus came to heal those who are hurt. He promises to be gentle with the hurting and to provide what is needed: rest. Those in our care are bruised and broken children. They, too, need gentleness. They are bruised reeds—they will be angry, fearful, sad—but if our Savior can gently deal with our anger, fear, and sorrow, we must also deal gently with theirs. We must respond to them with what they need—love, compassion, tenderness, and boundaries—not harshness or anger.

God is Present

"It is the LORD who goes before you. He will be with you; he will not leave you or forsake you. Do not fear or be dismayed" (Deuteronomy 31:8).

Our Father's promise is constant presence. No matter what happens or what we do, He won't leave us. We live in the truth of His unending love for us, not in the fear of His wrath. A child needs to know that they can't misbehave enough to be abandoned.

Once attachment is established, they will obey out of a response of love, rather than a fear of abandonment.

God Guides Us

"Even though I walk through the valley of the shadow of death, I will fear no evil, for you are with me; your rod and your staff, they comfort me" (Psalm 23:4).

So too the "rod" we use for a child isn't a stick that we beat them with. It's the gentle guidance and direction that we give them. It's the boundaries and rules we provide for them to keep them safe. We do need to provide direction, rules, and boundaries for our children—they can't make the rules or do whatever they want, however, we do this by being near them and helping them to stay on the path. God's rod is a rod of guidance. The rod guides the sheep in the way to go, providing boundaries and direction. Only an uncaring shepherd would allow his flock to wander without direction. Shepherds don't hit their sheep with a rod. They provide guidance by gently directing the sheep.

STOPLIGHT REFLECTIONS

1. Think back to your own childhood. Do you think you were securely attached to your own caregivers? What decisions by your parents led to this level of attachment?

2. Reflect on your own parenting. Do your children seem to have a secure attachment with you as a parent? What can you do to strengthen that attachment? How can you make time in your schedule to ensure you're making a vital connection with your kids? Set goals—such as a planned amount of time each day to spend quality time with your child, or a special outing each month.

Consider what both a secure and an insecure attachment

might look like after each of these incidents: a child falls over, is crying in the night, is vomiting, or gets stung by a bee. As a parent, how would you feel in each situation? What would the behavior of the child in each situation tell you about what they are feeling?

3. If you have a child who was adopted, how is creating attachment with him or her different from what it looks like with your biological children?

4. Talk about the different roles parents play in a child's life. You're a playmate, engaging in play with your children. You are a caregiver, feeding, clothing and providing care. You're a teacher, helping your child develop new skills. You're also a disciplinarian, setting boundaries for your child.

    Of the parents you know and interact with, which ones would you say excel at these different parenting roles? Go through each role and identify friends who are strong in those areas.

Prayer

Father, Son, and Holy Spirit, You have lived in relationship with each other for all of eternity! You made us in Your image, made for relationship with You. Thank You that You are always there for me when I am sick, lonely, or in need. When I turn from You, You restore me with Your love. Help me to trust Your unfailing goodness to me! Give me Your presence that I may love my children as You love me.

CHAPTER 4

Reality and Resilience

I HAD ONLY BEEN HOME FROM THE HOSPITAL for two weeks, just having had a C-section for my third child, Thomas. Tired and exhausted, my new, eleven-pound, colicky baby was constantly crying—and it seemed like there was nothing I could do to help. I was living life in Yellow Brain. At best. Much of the time, I felt like I was just struggling to survive.

Joshua, only two years old at the time, was playing quietly with some blocks on the floor while I held Thomas in my arms. Catherine, my four-year-old, came to me and asked for a glass of milk. Putting Thomas down in his baby seat on the floor, I was gone for a mere minute—but it was long enough to hear a crash and an unending, piercing scream. I rushed to the living room to find Thomas lying in the pile of blocks, with Joshua standing next to him.

I freaked out. *Mama is in Red Brain.*

Quickly I picked up Thomas. I pulled Joshua away from his

blocks and just . . . started yelling at him. "What are you doing?" I shouted. "Why did you pick him up? What were you thinking? You just . . . You just dropped him on the floor!"

Joshua's eyes were filled with terror. I could almost read the thoughts that were going through his mind. *Who is this monster? I'm scared. Is she going to hurt me?*

As Joshua burst into tears, he replied sheepishly, "I . . . I just wanted him to play with me . . ."

I walked into my room and stood looking in the mirror, the baby still screaming in my ear. Gently bouncing Thomas up and down, unable to soothe him, I looked at myself. *Where did that monster come from? How could I respond to my two-year-old son like that? He wasn't trying to do something wrong. I'm a horrible parent! What's wrong with me?*

Can you relate? We can often react to situations and not understand why we behave the way we do. In an instant we may find ourselves raising our voices, saying harsh words, or doing things we immediately regret.

When I saw Joshua hurting my newborn baby—a Red situation—I immediately flipped to Red. The mirroring systems of our socially-wired brains make behaviors and situations contagious. Our brains have the ability to reflect the behaviors around us. If you see Red, you go to Red.

This effect is quite evident when you walk into your child's room and see it in a complete mess, instantly putting you into Red Brain. You proceed to storm out of the room to find your son, giving him a lengthy and thorough lecture. Your son responds by storming off to his room and slamming the door. Now he is also in Red Brain, reflecting the situation he was just put in by your harsh words.

When an individual is in Red Brain, their actions and words make it easy for other people around them to move into Red Brain.

But Green is contagious, as well, particularly if parents are intentional about getting their kids into a safe, calm state.

In other words, Stoplight starts with you!

Trending Red

Why can't we stop shifting to Red? It's a question most parents ask themselves, whether they use the language of Stoplight or not. Why do we react the way we do in stressful situations? Why am I always freaking out during the chaotic moments of family life?

It's probably no surprise to learn that situations out of our control (or that we have little control over) can contribute to our ability to stay in Green Brain or to flip into Red Brain. If you were unable to sleep last night, you are likely to have less patience with your daughter when she comes home after school in dirty clothes. If you are experiencing unemployment, unsure where your next house payment will come from, you may find your spouse's comments are less funny and more irritating, often resulting in heated arguments before bed.

Sleep Deprivation

Most parents tend to stay up late after having put younger children to bed. During this time, parents may be taking time for themselves or completing tasks that didn't get accomplished during the day. As a result, parents often become sleep deprived during the early years of raising children. This lack of sleep deeply affects their ability to remain in Green Brain when they are spending time with their children during the day. A proper and healthy amount of sleep is a more important consideration than you may realize.

Stress

We speak lightly of this problem at times, but it's important to remember how ongoing stress and a perceived loss of control can be a significant factor in fueling our parenting responses. Problems at work, moving to a new home, losing a loved one, schooling challenges—these can all contribute to a flip to Red.

Uncertainty

When expecting a child, you have an image of what parenting will be like. When the baby arrives, it may not be what you had anticipated. Perhaps it is more self-sacrificial than you realized. Having to constantly hold, feed, and care for an infant may be more exhausting than you had anticipated. Breastfeeding may be more painful than you had first thought, and you may not feel your love reciprocated. Stress increases and a feeling of losing control abounds. You may even question your ability to properly care for and love your child.

These contributing circumstances are important to be aware of so that we can better manage our actions and emotions. Unfortunately, our current situations and surroundings are not the only things affecting our behaviors. Our past experiences can also have a very present and substantial effect on our actions, even influencing the way we parent. Your childhood still affects you today. A negative experience that made you feel unsafe as a child may result in a flip into Red Brain when you encounter something similar, causing others around you to also feel unsafe.

An Opportunity for Training?

You are tired. Life at work is hectic and stressful these days, and you can't seem to leave your work *at* work for the night. Your boss is breathing down your neck about every assignment, and your coworkers are staying clear of you because they don't want to be his next target. At home, the kids just started summer holidays, so the house is a mess, and your wife is stressed out because she has been with them all day.

You go upstairs to have a shower, only to find out that the hot water heater apparently isn't working.

You hear the kids playing. You go outside to check in with them and notice that they have taken most every towel and sheet from the house to make a fort, dragging the clean linen through the dirt and grass as they construct their masterpiece.

With all that is happening in your life, what is your perception in that moment as you look out at your kids building their fort? Do you see dirty linens or happy children? Creativity or thoughtlessness? Work that must be done (and redone) or an opportunity to train your children?

If we have low resilience in those moments, we will tend to lean toward having a frustrated response, focusing on the effect our kids' actions have on us. *I have thoughtless children who are doing nothing but making work for me, and therefore they must be sent to their rooms!*

With higher resilience, we can see the situation with the focus on our children. *I have creative children who are having fun using their imagination! Yes, the mess is inconvenient to me, but now I can use this as a training opportunity to teach my kids how to wash linens.*

Building Resilience

Yet past experiences can also make us stronger. They have likely built into us a certain level of resilience, the ability to endure hard experiences and to learn and grow from them. How your resilience was built up or torn down shapes and forms who you are today as a parent. Your past experiences, both negative and positive, help to develop your current resilience level.

But that level is always changing. Like a bank account, you can fill it up or empty it out depending on the day, situation, or emotional state. You have the power to refuel your resilience and the resilience of your children.

Many parents make their parenting decisions in the same way they were parented. When your kids were young, you might have tried new methods, reading various parenting books with the goal of being the best parent on the block. At the end of the day, though, we resort back to what we knew growing up, whether it is incentives such as behavior charts and rewards, or correction such as time-outs and taking away privileges. Yelling, shaming, and physical aggression may also have been part of what we grew up with and something we slip into in our own parenting.

I must emphasize that I am not saying that you or your parents have failed and that there is no hope for the future. Your parents knew no different, and they were trying to do what was best for you. You knew no different, and you are only trying to do what is best for your children.

I was the same way. Even now, after years of research and developing the Stoplight Approach, I sometimes find myself falling back into the parenting methods I grew up with. I have to stop myself and reflect on the kind of parent I really want to be.

And even if you are new to the Stoplight understanding, it's not too late to change your own and your children's resilience levels. It won't happen overnight, but it is possible to adjust your habits and parenting practices, which improves your perseverance and resilience.

There are three factors in effectively building resilience. The higher we are in these factors, the more capacity our children have for building resilience. These factors are the "I have," the "I am," and the "I can" factors.

Having a high "I have" factor means you have support, structure, and a safe environment around you. Think about your own "I have" factor, especially during your childhood. Who were your safe people and what was your safe place as you grew up?

A high "I am" factor means you have identity and self-worth.

Who encouraged you and poured truth into your life? How did they do that?

A high "I can" factor means you have positive coping mechanisms for dealing with challenges and stressful situations. What skills did you grow up feeling confident in? Who helped you learn them? Were you encouraged to pursue your passions?

These three factors are built up over time in kids as parents create environments of safety, value, and acceptance. Like a bank account, you can fill it up, or you can empty it out. Over time, if you aren't careful, resilience levels can begin to look quite low, in both parents and in children.

Personally, I know that if I'm not taking time to rest, laugh, and have fun, I forget my self-worth, my "I am" factor, and I slip into Yellow Brain. Down goes my resilience level! Or, if I'm not meeting with safe friends who encourage me, I'm missing my "I have" factor, and I can easily flip to Red Brain.

When our resilience level is low, we tend to live mainly in Yellow or Red Brain because we feel unloved, undervalued, and unsafe. Building into those two factors brings us back to Green because we are strengthening our "I can" factor in the process. Sometimes, though, we recognize our low resilience, but we simply don't want to (or don't feel we can) build it up.

Do you ever feel so depleted that all you want to do is hide away and eat chocolate? You don't want to talk to a friend, go to a counselor, or pray—all you want to do is block out the rest of the world? You would be surprised at how many parents feel this way, some on a daily basis.

It can be difficult to make a move, but it is in those depleted moments that we need to be building into our three resilience factors. You are unsafe to yourself, your spouse, and your children when you are living in a state of Yellow and Red. Building resilience in yourself will help increase the resilience in your children because you can focus on them while still feeling confident in your own life. With a high level of resilience, your perception of each situation changes, and you're back in Green Brain!

Baby Steps to Resilience

Like a bank account grows through many small deposits, building up resilience levels requires many small contributions. This doesn't happen overnight, but it does happen every day.

The "I Have" Factor

Who are the safe people you can trust and who can help draw you closer to God? These are people who will challenge you and help you grow in your relationships with God. Everyone needs a godly mentor!

In order to grow my own "I have" factors, I have four different people who build into my life and challenge me in different ways. I have also recognized that I need to have structures and routines put into place to create safe spaces in my life. I can have family night prayers. I can have predictability. I can decide to go on a date with my husband. I can create a healthy family culture. I can make Green choices about when I go to sleep at night (which I've found is the biggest contributing factor in sending me into Yellow or Red!).

The "I Am" Factor

As I first started understanding the principles behind the Stoplight Approach, something that became very clear was that I did not see myself as God sees me. One day, I heard an impactful sermon by Reverend John Armitage in which he said, "Love God, love yourself, love others." In that moment, I realized that I really didn't love myself the way God loves me. Had I ever?

If we don't love ourselves as God loves us, we cause our resilience to become depleted. My Stoplight will be flashing a big, bright yellow circle, and I will not be able to love others and build relationships with them. What's more, even though I try to love others, they may not feel that love when I am in Yellow.

I can't love others without loving God first! If I don't love God first, I won't see others *through God's eyes*.

How can I build a relationship with someone if I don't love myself and understand what true, unconditional love is?

Now, by "love yourself," I don't mean a self-centered love like the world promotes. I mean seeing myself the way God sees me. I am lovable. Despite my mistakes, God still delights in me. The love I have for myself is a mirror image of how He sees me. I need to see myself through God's reflection, not the world's reflection.

The "I Can" Factor

I need God to help me. I need support and encouragement. I need to take baby steps. I need to be going forward and not going back, and as I go forward, I need to look for mentors who can help me get on track and stay on track.

Life isn't easy. Difficult situations will always be present. However, these challenges are more easily faced when we are constantly building up our resilience.

> I know how to be brought low, and I know how to
> abound. In any and every circumstance, I have learned the
> secret of facing plenty and hunger, abundance and need.
> I can do all things through him who strengthens me.
> PHILIPPIANS 4:12-13

A Model of Resilience

Resilience—the ability to endure hard experiences and learn and grow from them—can be seen over and over again throughout the Bible, in the stories of people who lived through unimaginable hardship and yet were able to maintain faith and trust in God, allowing Him to bring good out of their awful circumstances.

One of the clearest examples of this is in the life of Paul. As a first-century Christian and missionary, Paul was constantly persecuted by the Roman government and the Jewish authorities who did not want him spreading the gospel. To say he suffered through a lot is an understatement:

> Five times I received at the hands of the Jews the forty
> lashes less one. Three times I was beaten with rods. Once
> I was stoned. Three times I was shipwrecked; a night
> and a day I was adrift at sea; on frequent journeys, in
> danger from rivers, danger from robbers, danger from
> my own people, danger from Gentiles, danger in the
> city, danger in the wilderness, danger at sea, danger from
> false brothers; in toil and hardship, through many a
> sleepless night, in hunger and thirst, often without food,
> in cold and exposure. And, apart from other things,
> there is the daily pressure on me of my anxiety for all
> the churches.
>
> 2 CORINTHIANS 11:24-28

With this in mind, we can read Philippians 4 with a better appreciation of Paul's first-hand experience with suffering: "Not that I am speaking of being in need, for I have learned in whatever situation I am to be content. I know how to be brought low, and I know how to abound. In any and every circumstance, I have learned the secret of facing plenty and hunger, abundance and need" (Philippians 4:11-12).

How is Paul able to have this resilience in the midst of such a

Red situation? Look at what he says immediately after describing his hardships: "I can do all things through him who strengthens me" (Philippians 4:13).

Paul's dependence on Christ is the basis of his resilience; it allows him to endure, gives him the hope to continue, and strengthens him to face new challenges. Like Paul, we too can learn from Jesus and draw strength from His love and peace, allowing Him to build our own resilience. As we teach our children to depend on the love of their Father in heaven, we help them increase their own resilience in facing challenges.

We increase our resilience by building our "I have," our "I am," and our "I can" factors. As Christians, we have a major advantage. We have the very life of Christ within us, and as we receive from Him daily, the depth of these key factors grows:

I have—I have a relationship with God. I have safety in God. I have a role model in Jesus Christ. I have a consistent relationship with One who will never leave me.

I am—I am loved. I am valued by God. I am God's masterpiece. I am made in God's image. I am forgiven.

I can—With the help of the Holy Spirit, I can make changes for the better in my life. I can interact with my community of fellow believers. I can communicate with God. I can be a part of building God's Kingdom.

In the story of Paul, we see the life-changing effects of one individual's resilience, strengthened by an understanding of who he was in God's eyes. Paul was able to spread the good news of Jesus to people far and wide despite strong adversity. We, too, can have that relationship with God, and that same potential for increased resilience.

If our identity is in the God who sees as we really are, He will give us strength.

STOPLIGHT REFLECTIONS

1. What is a situation in your life right now that is causing you to feel an increase of stress or feel a loss of control? Is that situation affecting how you react and respond to those around you—especially your spouse and children?

2. How are you going to be intentional at finding ways to build your own "I have," "I am," and "I can" factors? How can you do this for your children?

3. Where are you getting your resilience from? Make a list of the ways you have seen God impact your "I have," "I am," and "I can" factors.

4. As you go through this day, pause to place your hand on your chest and pray to God: "Your presence fills me. Your presence is love." Change the last word of this prayer throughout the day—"Your presence is: love, peace, patience, strength." As you do, let Christ calm you, and give Himself to you.

Prayer

Jesus, thank You for living in me! You understand my challenges,
for You lived on this earth as I do. As You heard Your Father,
help me hear Your voice of love. From that place of love,
give me the resilience I need for each day.

CHAPTER 5

Triggers from the Past

A NUMBER OF YEARS AGO I was faced with an overwhelming situation, one in which my brain could not process the information in a healthy way. I witnessed the ongoing abuse of vulnerable children where I lived in Uganda. My ability to intervene was limited, but I did what I could. I tried harder and harder to make a difference, yet so much was completely out of my control. I couldn't change people. I couldn't change their decisions. I felt powerless and helpless.

Unfortunately, I didn't talk to anyone, so I didn't process those feelings in a healthy way. I just packed them deep inside me. Their intensity increased, and I started having nightmares and flashbacks. I slept very little. I looked OK during the day, but the nights were horrible. The stress became so intense that I was unable to eat, losing weight to the point where I became deathly sick. I was diagnosed with Post Traumatic Stress Disorder. The journey toward recovery has been long and difficult.

Why did this affect me so badly? I asked myself this question often. Others had been witnesses to this awful situation, and while equally horrified, they did not have the same symptoms and become critically ill like me.

I later understood that the situation with the abused children was a sort of trigger for me, fueling flashbacks to my own past. While my childhood was overall very different than what these poor kids were experiencing, there were some specific similarities that were enough to drive these intense memories to the surface. I grew up in a home that I believed demanded perfection of me. I felt that my parents' approval and happiness was conditional upon my performance, and that I could never meet their standards. I struggled to make them proud of me but never felt I matched up. Instead, I only felt their criticism.

As a young girl who struggled in school because of learning disabilities, I wasn't successful in academics and was often bullied or rejected by my peers. Powerless and often helpless to change situations, I was insecure about my worth and value. Yet I still wanted to prove to everyone I was good enough.

With hard work and focus, I did well at university. As long as I had everything in "control," I could hide the feelings of insecurity. And for many years I did. But those feelings were still there, nonetheless.

Now, facing the abusive treatment of children that continued despite my best efforts to intervene, the situation triggered the helplessness, powerlessness, and worthlessness I felt as a child. Although rationally I knew the hurt those children experienced wasn't my fault, what I internalized was something like, *I'm just not good enough, and that is why they are still being hurt.* I needed a way to cope with this incredible burden of guilt, and the overwhelming emotions that this guilt initiated.

But my Red Brain wasn't very logical, and the choices I made when I was in Red Brain weren't always the most productive or healthy. I was carrying a burden I was never meant to carry. I needed a place to put the guilt and overwhelming emotions. I saw a trauma specialist who gave me skills to deal with the pain, but I couldn't vanquish the emotions, no matter how hard I repeated those techniques.

I needed to release those burdens at the foot of the Cross. Every flashback. Every nightmare. Everything that I was powerless to control. It was only when I gave my burdens to Jesus that I was able to be released from the weight and the pain. "Keep my soul; deliver me," was my mantra.

Sometimes I want to take the burdens back. But I need to realize those times when my past trauma has been triggered, sending me into Yellow or Red Brain. And I have to surrender to Jesus all that is holding me back.

The Present Effects of Past Red

This is an extreme example of how our past can influence our present. So many times we quickly flip into Red Brain, and later look back and think, *Wow! What happened to me? It wasn't really that big a deal, but I reacted like it was a life-and-death situation.*

Your son leaves his toys out, and instead of calmly working on clean-up skills, you find yourself angrily throwing his precious Lego creations into the box with pieces haphazardly flying apart. Your spouse makes an off-hand remark, and instead of pausing to determine what they actually meant, you are suddenly slamming doors and crying into your pillow. Your teenager complains about washing the dishes, you feel the anger rising, and a dozen inappropriate words immediately come to mind.

What is pushing your buttons? When you overreact to a situation, and you find yourself flipping to Red Brain, that is your cue that it is time for some investigation and self-reflection. On the surface you may be able to find a reason—you didn't get a good night's sleep, or work is really stressful right now—but there may be something else at the root of that reaction if you can observe a pattern. If our buttons are getting pushed, we need to figure out what that button is, how it gets pushed, and what to do about it!

What Buttons Do You Have?

Remember, Red means stop, so if you find yourself in Red, not only do you need to stop in the moment, but after you are back in Green, you need to continue pausing to reflect on what put you in Red. Whether there are gaping holes from adverse childhood experiences such as abuse or parental divorce, or irritating sores from a comment that cut deep, you need to discover what your buttons are and begin the work of healing. We often normalize or minimize our bad experiences. But old wounds need real healing, not a quick Band-Aid.

Be aware of your childhood. Were your parents present? Were they overly strict? Did you have frequent moves? Were you exposed to violence or abuse (physical, sexual, emotional, etc.)? Reflect on major life events. Were there any deaths in your life? Major accidents? Serious illnesses?

Ask yourself, "Why?" three times as a sort of pathfinding mission to discover the roots of your trigger. For example: If you flipped to Red over the toy incident, ask yourself, *Why did the toys being left out stress me so?* Because it made the house messy. *Why does the house being messy stress me?* Because I feel out of control when there is a mess. *Why do I feel out of control when there is a mess?* Because if I can't control the mess outside of me, maybe I can't control the mess inside of me, and that means I'm not good enough. Identifying our buttons may be work we can do on our own, but sometimes a wise friend or a professional counselor is necessary as you do this important work.

Why do certain words or actions push us into Red? Sometimes it is obvious. If you were bitten by a dog as a child, you know why the very sight of a dog scares you. But these sorts of triggers can also be very subtle, the connection less clear. A trigger may be a sound, word, item, or facial expression—anything that somehow reminds you of the Red situation you experienced. For example, if you were attacked or bullied under an orange tree, the smell of that tree's flowers could send you into Red Brain, even if you don't consciously remember that the assault occurred under an orange tree. Or if your husband comes home from work to a messy house and asks what you've been doing all day, it could trigger feelings of worthlessness. Identifying what your triggers are will help you learn to remain in Green Brain when the triggers show up unexpectedly.

I have often struggled with going into Yellow or Red when my children do something to embarrass me while we are out and about—as tends to occur when I feel like I've lost control. This happens when we are in a public place or at a special event and I can't get them to do as I please—like a screaming tantrum in the middle of church! My image is being soiled because I feel like a failure.

Really, I feel *powerless*. Like the time my five-year-old child forgot to put underwear on at the Christmas concert, and his zipper happened to fall down. (I thought, *What kind of horrible mom am I?*) Or the time my four-year-old pooped in the swimming pool. (I felt awful!) Or all the times my kids didn't dress themselves appropriately for the weather.

You know these moments, I'm sure. There's the child who screams in the grocery store, forcing you to leave a full cart of groceries and storm home in a Yellow-Red haze. There is the teenager who called you stupid and is rude and disrespectful. Or the child who refuses to clean their room when company is coming over. The embarrassment is difficult to deal with. *What does this reveal about me?*

I grew up in a world where image mattered. What people thought was so important. I have to remember that I'm playing to an audience of one. I need to put blinders on. I need to do what's right for my child and not to please the audience. It does not matter what others think. All that matters is what God thinks. I need to look at my child in the way God does in that moment.

How to Disable a Button!

It will take planning, time, and hard work to learn not to respond when your buttons get pushed. There are neural connections in your brain that cause you to react based on past experiences and behaviors modeled for you before. It is necessary to use intentional, consistent, persistent thoughts and actions to overcome these easy, automatic reactions and create a new neural pathway. Here are some ways to get started:

A 'Counter-Narrative' Box

At the root of many buttons are lies we believe about ourselves. Identifying and exposing these lies for what they are is an effective way to disarm a button. For instance, you may feel, "I was a bad child. That is why I was punished so much."

When an adult hurts a child, it is never the child's fault. No child deserves to be hurt. But your inner voices will continue to speak lies and try to get you to believe you are to blame. We must learn to recognize lies and replace lies with truth: "I am strong. I am valuable. I am loved. I am unique." On small pieces of paper, write down all of the lies you are believing. These could be lies you hear inside of yourself, lies you assume other people are thinking of you, or even lies people have said about you. On the backside of the papers, write down the counter-narratives—what the truth is. Put all of these in a small box and keep the box close to you. Personally, I write Bible verses as my counter-narratives, and I keep my box next to my bed.

Breathing and Reflection

Breathing can release stress, give us a new perspective, control anger, manage pain, create awareness, and calm the body—if it is done right. Remember, when we are in Red Brain, our bodies go into a sort of survival mode. Our heart races, our pupils dilate, and our breaths become short and shallow. The hormones that are released can be managed by taking deep and controlled breaths. It almost seems too easy!

Practice deep breathing while visualizing yourself in a different situation. It will become muscle memory, responding through breathing when your life becomes overwhelming.

You can also practice breathing with your kids. An easy and fun way is to pretend to blow up a balloon, using your hands to show how big your balloon is growing. It will help calm them down without even realizing it.

Wise Counsel

According to Heather Forbes, LCSW, the most effective way to change the negative patterns of the brain—especially those that have been created by past adverse experiences—is through safe, nurturing, human connection. Finding and being accountable to a safe person or community with which you can be vulnerable is a powerful way to encourage healing and progress.[1]

Parents can be this community support for each other. You can have a Green home only if the parents are in Green Brain; therefore, a community of fellow parents can really help each other stay in Green Brain!

A good friend, a mentor, an older person you trust, or a

spiritual leader who can listen, love, and support you can be helpful. Someone who can give you a different perspective can walk alongside you as you process your past. Healing can be a long process. Unfortunately, that pathway to Red Brain will always be there; however, with the help of others, we can learn to recognize our buttons and triggers and consistently follow our plan to avoid sliding into Red Brain. If needed, find a trained counselor who can help you appropriately deal with the past and respond to your present pain.

Practicing Gratitude

It can be natural to focus on the negative parts of our lives, especially when we have been affected by past Red experiences. However, taking moments to be grateful for the positive and life-giving parts of your life can be very helpful in the healing process.

So intentionally notice and reflect upon what has gone well each day. Focus on the Green, even in the midst of Red. Your spouse's sense of humor, your children's health, your parents' support—there is always something to be thankful for.

Children with Red Shadows

When we first adopted Beth, she would lash out and react vocally when she went into Red Brain, which was very often. People who met her were welcomed with lots of love and friendliness, but once they tried to get close to her, she would immediately push them away. She seemed outgoing and energetic, but she could jump from Green Brain to Red Brain at a moment's notice, and everyone knew it. Even now that she is twelve, Beth shows everyone just how she feels.

When we first adopted Jessica, she would disassociate herself from any situation where people were getting in trouble. To anyone watching from afar, it looked as if she was daydreaming. She was using it as a coping mechanism she had found worked just fine for her—physically she was present, but in every other way, she had left the situation. Interestingly, Jessica also got extremely upset whenever she felt alone. Yes, she could check out of a situation, but she still needed the company and comfort of people.

I have two children who have experienced past trauma, but outwardly it looks completely different for each of them.

And, as many adoptive parents understand, these kids have buttons and triggers too—situations that will cause them to behave in certain ways because past experiences have shaped their brain development.

Often, we do not realize how much children may have been shaped by traumatic moments in their past. It's important to look beyond the child's behavior, because only when you understand the underlying issue can you treat it effectively. Addressing only the behavior issue is like applying a bandage without properly treating the wound and giving it the attention it needs for healing.

One thing that often goes unnoticed or unidentified in children is the level of stress they are experiencing. Many kids these days live with constant low-level stress. This stress and anxiety decreases their window of stress tolerance, which is a fancy way to say that they don't have the reserves to cope well with a little more additional stress.

We need to understand that the emotion that has been triggered is real in the perception of the child, even if there is no objectively threatening situation.

Two people who are going through the same event can interpret it very differently. That can be true for adults, of course, as well. For example, when there is a bat in my bedroom, I am yelling and screaming and extremely terrified, feeling very threatened and unsafe. But then my seventeen-year-old son comes into the room with a racket and goes after the bat without any change in his emotional or physiological state.

"See, Mom, it's friendly!"

Sometimes, it's not about the truth of an event; it's about one's perception of it. Often parents don't see this with their kids. You, as a parent, may think the event is normal and safe, but for the child, it may be traumatic.

Most parents would agree that house fires, war, or sexual abuse are examples of objectively traumatic events. But we must be aware that some kinds of "normal" life events can also be traumatic for kids, such as medical procedures or thunderstorms, being left alone, etc. These everyday events may be amplified into a threat by a child's perceived lack of preparedness for what's about to happen, such as the absence of a caregiver.

The younger the child, the more vulnerable they are to trauma, as they have limited abilities to protect themselves and so are more easily overwhelmed. Trauma in the womb, such as drug and alcohol use by the mother, can result in the child being born overwhelmed. The infant brain becomes hyper-alert to perceived danger. In other words, the brain becomes programmed in such a way that feelings of terror and helplessness become a normal state of being. It's not about how big the traumatic event was, but rather the child's perception of how threatening the event felt. According to Dr. Dan Siegel, when infants and young children experience threats of violence that are chronic and occur early enough, the stage is set for a host of learning and behavior problems.[2]

For a person who has been traumatized, the Green Brain is very often simply unable to calm the fear response of the Red Brain. As explained by Dr. Bruce Perry in *The Boy Who Was Raised as a Dog*, this inability to calm down means that there will be some other way to deal with the extreme emotions—acting out aggressively, suffering silently from overwhelming feelings, or completely blanking out from the distressing fear-response signals. They are unable to handle their own emotions due to certain pathways having developed in their brain and are unable to behave in a logical, ideal way.[3]

While it cannot erase the past, the Stoplight language can help you and your children understand and process past Red situations. When these triggers surface, recognize and identify these events and emotions as Red or Yellow. By putting words to the situation, parents give kids the tools to begin having some control.

Given the brain's capacity for change, every child can experience healing from a traumatic past, as new neural pathways are created within the safety of a consistently loving environment. Instead of letting a traumatic background define you or your children, look at it as an opportunity to learn and grow as a Stoplight family.

It is a long journey with lots of ups and downs, and my family isn't finished yet. However, with understanding and love, we keep learning what buttons each of us are living with, what triggers them, and how to disarm them.

I have told you these things, so that in me you may have
peace. In this world you will have trouble. But take heart!
I have overcome the world.

JOHN 16:33

Storms of Life

And in the fourth watch of the night, he came to them,
walking on the sea. But when the disciples saw him
walking on the sea, they were terrified, and said, "It is a
ghost!" and they cried out in fear. But immediately Jesus
spoke to them, saying, "Take heart; it is I. Do not be
afraid."

And Peter answered him, "Lord, if it is you, command
me to come to you on the water." He said, "Come." So
Peter got out of the boat and walked on the water and
came to Jesus. But when he saw the wind, he was afraid,
and beginning to sink he cried out, "Lord, save me." Jesus
immediately reached out his hand and took hold of him,
saying to him, "O you of little faith, why did you doubt?"
And when they got into the boat, the wind ceased. And
those in the boat worshiped him, saying, "Truly you are
the Son of God."

MATTHEW 14:25-33

Like Peter, we all experience storms at times, whether they
be financial, emotional, or physical. These storms make life feel
out of control, and they have the potential to drive us into Red
Brain.

Sometimes we can take steps to avoid a specific storm, but
many of them are inevitable. All we can do is choose how we will
respond to them. We have two choices in how to respond to these
storms: We can focus on the storm and allow it to keep us in Red,

or we can refuse to the let the storm control our life and instead try to move back to Green.

The account of Jesus walking on the water shows us how Peter used both responses. In the beginning, he is focused on Jesus. In Green Brain, despite the storm, Peter is ready to learn new things and push his faith to its boundaries. He steps out of the boat, and an amazing thing happens—he is able to walk on top of the water.

But not for long. Peter soon allows the storm to become his focus. He sees the crashing waves, feels the pelting rain, and hears the roaring wind. As feelings of fear overwhelm him, Peter focuses less and less on Jesus and more on the stressors around him. It is at this point that he begins to sink.

The same happens to us. When life gets hectic—someone is sick, bills pile up, work demands more and more hours—often our time with God is the first thing to go. As with Peter, it's not a conscious decision, but little by little, if we're not careful, our focus shifts away from Jesus and toward the pressing troubles. It's never too late to turn back to God. When Peter realized his mistake, he cried out to God for help, and Jesus reached out and took his hand.

With help from God, we will be better equipped to handle the situation. Spending time with God can help us redefine success, concentrating on the important things in life—not "having a nicer car than my neighbor," but "loving my neighbor as myself." We can also pray, asking God to show us where we can simplify our lives. Focusing on God will not always make our problems magically disappear—after all, the storm didn't immediately dissipate when Peter stepped out of the boat—but it will allow us to not overcome by the troubles, because we know we can trust in God and use His guidance to navigate the storm.

Like walking on water, parenting well can feel impossible at times. The truth is, we need God's help. So when Red situations seem to be overwhelming, stop, breathe, and ask God for help.

STOPLIGHT REFLECTIONS

1. Think back to a time you recently flipped into Red. Can you trace back to the root cause of this reaction by asking yourself three "why?" questions? Can you think of other times that same trigger caused you to flip to Red?

2. Next time you encounter that trigger, how can you plan ahead to manage that moment and stay in Green Brain? Remember to give yourself grace if it takes a while to learn how to avoid flipping to Red when that particular button gets pushed!

3. Stop and consider what buttons are being pushed by your children. Ask God to reveal anything in your life that needs healing. Brainstorm ways you can stay in Green.

4. Find a quiet place to read Matthew 14:25-33 aloud slowly, imagining the sound of the storm, the feel of the waves splashing, the terror of the disciples. As you read it, what words leap out at you? Where are you in that story? What is God saying to you?

—————————————— *Prayer* ——————————————

Loving God, I grieve for the brokenness of this world. I turn to You, for You are the healer. Show me the lies that hold me back from living freely in Your grace; help me replace those lies with Your healing truth. Mend my wounded places and give me wisdom and compassion for the places of hurt in my own children.

CHAPTER 6

Future Plans: Staying Green

My son Peter had his first seizure when he was two years old. My husband was out of town, and my fourteen-year-old daughter, Catherine, left early to walk the younger kids to church so I could clean the house because we had visitors coming over after church. It had already been a crazy morning by the time the kids left the house, and my stress level was rising.

Peter was sitting in Catherine's arms when the seizure happened. The whole service stopped to try to help him. When I finally arrived, I saw my usually energetic son lying on the ground, another son crying in the corner watching, and Catherine surrounded by my other girls in a frantic state. It was a horrific situation which I could not have dealt with properly without the support of my church. They gave me the strength to stay Green in a very, very Red situation.

Some church families took in my children for the day, others helped me get Peter to the hospital, and others prayed.

My whole life became about figuring out what had happened and what to do. I was in Red situation after Red situation and had to allow Green people to help me keep some semblance of calm.

I was in survival mode. It was an achievement to get my kids into bed at night. Without the calm influence of people who surrounded me at that time, I don't know how I would have coped. They helped me to laugh—to see the humor in the dog licking the highchair that I was too busy and stressed to clean. My life was Red. I couldn't walk away from it, but the community around me kept bringing me back to Green.

It can be easy to fall into Red Brain, but getting back up to Green takes hard work, patience, and perseverance.

Yes, Stoplight starts with you, but what do you do when the day you are living in is Red, Red, RED, and it's a situation that you cannot escape, a situation that you have zero control over?

Even when we proactively build our resilience and manage our triggers, we will still have days when everything feels Red around us. Your spouse may be traveling, and the children are sick. You have a colicky baby that won't stop crying. You have guests coming, the house is a mess, and you haven't made dinner.

Maybe your life as a whole is in an ongoing Red situation. Your spouse just walked out on you, so now you are a single parent, and you don't have money to pay for rent. Maybe your child has just been diagnosed with cancer. Maybe you are a refugee family living without a country. Maybe you have a child with special needs who is not growing and acting like other children.

If you can't get out of the situation, then you just have to live through it. How? It's not about having the tools; it's about first understanding the situation.

When you're living in Red, you need to stop, simplify, and redefine success.

Just Stop!

Remember, Red means "Stop!" For a time, stop trying to solve the problem. Stop the task you are doing. Stop the conversation. Stop everything, because to carry on would be unsafe and unproductive. You'll never get to Green by stewing in Red.

Name It Red

"Name It to Tame It" is a strategy that Dr. Dan Siegel promotes. Name the emotion you are feeling. Be specific, if you can, because clear language helps you focus, calming your body and reducing the physiological reactions that occur.

Sometimes, you are not able to name the exact emotion that you are feeling. The colors of the Stoplight Approach give us an easy way to identify emotions. You start by recognizing the brain state you are in. You feel on edge but can't name the emotion as nervousness or anxiety. You can simply say, "Right now, I feel

Yellow." Or maybe you feel overwhelming anger or anxiety: "Right now, I am in Red."

Labeling the brain state you are in makes it easier to get back to Green Brain by allowing you to think more clearly about the situation and react in a logical way.

Pause to Breathe

Take deep breaths. This gets oxygen to your brain and helps your ability to think so that you can get back to Green. Slow breathing is important! In Red Brain you have a decreased blood oxygen level, so by enhancing oxygen flow to your brain you can help to physiologically bring yourself back to a more stable brain state.

Take a deep breath. Now count to four and let out the breath slowly. Repeat this until you feel calm. By stopping and breathing, you stop the spiral that takes place when you go into Red Brain. It's important to practice this method when you aren't in a stressful situation so that it will become a habit that you don't have to think about.

Use Your Green Plan

Plan for how you will safely get yourself back to Green. This planning ahead requires your full capacity, so it needs to be done ahead of time while you are in Green. Everyone is different, and this is your plan, but the goal should be to have a few simple, enjoyable moments that move you closer to Green Brain. Get a drink of water and a snack. Find a new room to relax in. Go for a walk, read a book, or put on some music.

Red people often struggle to play or laugh because it's *hard*, and it requires a lot of effort, but true play is a great way to get yourself back into Green Brain. You need to do some kind of self-care for yourself in order to be safe for your kids.

Reacting

Responding

Simplify Your Life and Redefine Success

The more pressures you have in life, the higher the likelihood you'll flip to Red Brain. Many of those pressures are self-inflicted and not always necessary. We feel our children need to be involved in different extracurricular activities, like tutoring, music, and sports. We get so occupied doing "good" things, such as volunteering at schools and churches, looking after the neighbor's cat, and doing our grandmother's washing, that we become overwhelmed. All of a sudden, our whole family is moving in the fast lane; there's no time for family dinners, game nights, or Sunday afternoon picnics. Now we have a family living in Yellow, where everyone is stressed and tired, no one is functioning at their best, and everyone is at risk of flipping to Red more easily.

Often we focus on ensuring that we are giving our children the best, but this can be to the detriment of ourselves and our family. If we're constantly rushing around to make things perfect, remaining calm is difficult. Although we have good motives, we're not really looking at the big perspective. Without being in Green Brain ourselves, we can't maintain a Green home. Simplify your life. Find ways to ensure that you're living in Green Brain because this is the example that your children will follow.

Sometimes we need to stop and refocus. Some periods in life can be more stressful than others, such as financial struggles, increased work intensity, moving house, or the hustle and bustle of the end or beginning of a school year. If you find yourself frequently and easily in Red Brain, it is probably a sign that you need to simplify your life by cutting back on activities.

The same applies to our kids—if we notice they are exhausted and in Red Brain, simplify their lives. This reduces the exhaustion and increases family time and time for play. If their rooms are full of clothes and toys, then it's difficult for them to keep their minds organized and calm. Help them understand that keeping their room clean will help calm their anxiety.

Toys go on holiday in our house. The only toys the kids get are the ones that can fit on the shelf. After a few weeks, we take away some of those toys and rotate other toys back in from storage. Our children function much better when they have less clutter in their room. We also take turns giving these toys away to children in need. When we lived in Uganda, it was very easy to bless those with less. Every so often, we had each child give away a toy to a child of their choice. Involve your children in giving to those in need!

What Is Success?

So often parenting feels like a competition. Who has the nicest house and the nicest car? Which children go to the best school? Coming out on top of these imaginary competitions may feel like success, temporarily at least, but seeing parenting as a competition isn't healthy because we're not looking at the best interests of our children. Your family needs your time and energy, not your money, high-end SUV, and superior front lawn.

We properly define success by having better, wiser expectations. Ask yourself what expectations you've put on yourself and your parenting—and how you might change them.

Facing the Red

Imagine there's a fire—a roaring, scorching, insatiable fire, raging out of control. Firefighters arrive on the scene. People are fleeing the burning building, and still more are trapped inside. If the firefighters are not able to control their own emotions, they are unable to think strategically and do their jobs. Consider the cool-headed emotions necessary to be able to run into a burning building while everyone else is running out. How are they able to stay in Green when there is Red all around? Because they are prepared, equipped, and have practiced prevention. The same must be true for us.

Be Prepared

Expect that fires will happen, and that they cannot be avoided. Understand that fires are a part of the job. Your child is not perfect, and neither are you, so dysfunctions will happen. Understanding and believing this will help to de-escalate your own emotions when there is an outburst. This is just a part of being a parent. It doesn't mean you have a bad child, or that you are a bad parent. It is not a direct reflection of you and your inabilities, but rather it is a part of growing and learning together in your relationship with your child.

Recognize Your Enemy

Red people in a Red environment say and do very harmful things. My natural tendency in my human flesh is to fight back—to protect and guard myself. I'm learning that the only way I can stay in Green is to recognize that I'm in a battle. But it's not a battle with my husband, who has come home from a business trip, jet-lagged and hungry. My enemy is not my child, who is being rude and disrespectful. My job is not my enemy, nor are the other people or responsibilities in my life. My enemy is Satan.

Until I went to Africa, I didn't really understand spiritual warfare. I had talked about it, but I never had truly felt it. The work of Satan can sometimes feel almost invisible in my polished, "civilized" life in Canada, but not so in Uganda, with its witchcraft and other forms of darkness so out in the open.

There were times living in Africa where I clearly felt the darkness and weight of evil, and I could feel it being lifted off me as I prayed and placed it at the foot of the Cross. The reality of spiritual warfare became very real to me.

We may not often realize that we're in a battle. But we are. When something isn't beautiful, good, or true, where is it coming from? It's Satan working in me and in my sin nature.

The Lord's prayer says, "Lead us not into temptation" (Matthew 6:13). Why do we pray this? Because we live in a world full of temptations, a world focused on its own selfish ambitions.

As parents, we face our own temptations every day. I'm tempted to get angry at my kids. I'm tempted to be on my phone instead of focusing on them. I'm tempted to be critical and judging.

Parents, we need to remember that our child is not our enemy! It might be that my child (or myself!) is in a tangled web of lies peddled by the evil one.

Our children face their own temptations. They are facing so many societal challenges, social media temptations, peer pressures, and worldly expectations. We are truly in a battle for our kids' lives! And just like being prepared for a fire, I need to be alert and have a plan in place. I need to be intentional with prayer because prayer is powerful.

I am in the process of learning to rely on God during these battles—and recognize that God is the one who needs to lead me into the battle.

Arm Yourself

Firefighters are not superheroes; they are fragile humans just like us. Their bodies are no more resistant to the dangers of a burning building than ours are. But because they are equipped with fireproof uniforms, smoke masks, and even a fire truck, they can do some extraordinary things that they cannot credit to their own abilities.

You, as a parent, are being asked to be a superhero every day for your children. Unlike superheroes, though, you do become tired, you do get angry, you don't always feel heroic, and you don't get the admiration and appreciation Superman does!

So you need to be equipped with the appropriate gear, the right strategies and correct knowledge of who your children are and what their history is. Know what your standards and values are as a parent and how you want to maintain those while parenting your child.

Remember that your child is either safe or unsafe, not good or bad. Don't discipline your child unless they are in Green Brain, where they can calmly understand the connection between behavior and consequences. If you can, go for a walk before addressing the situation, or ask your spouse to take over if you feel yourself flipping into Red Brain. Exercise helps so much! Run laps around the house with your kids to calm down.

We often expect our children to put out the fires, but we are the senior firefighters in this situation, so we need to take responsibility. You can't send a junior firefighter (a child) in alone, but you can work with them as a team and teach them how to douse flames. Your family needs to work together to learn how to handle the fires that will come your way.

Discovering the Roots of Behavior

My daughter Beth was not happy, and I didn't know why. It started with her hitting her siblings, and when I asked what was wrong, she ran off into the yard. I could have yelled after her, listing off all the things she was doing wrong, but I was keeping myself in Green Brain, recognizing that there was probably more to the story. So I made milkshakes for all my kids, and she came in to have one. A fun snack can often calm a child down.

"It seems like you feel unsafe right now," I said. "Can you explain what's wrong?"

That set her off again. "Why is Peter playing with my markers? And why does Rebecca have to come to our house! I hate Rebecca!"

Rebecca, an intern of mine, was going to be looking after the kids while I traveled for work and my husband was away on a business trip. The kids knew and loved Rebecca, so I didn't understand why this would set Beth off and make her so angry.

I stayed calm as I asked Beth to come up to my room to chat. As we walked into my room and I saw my suitcase on my bed, I started putting the pieces together. And it wasn't that complex of a puzzle: I didn't have a little girl who hated her siblings or our family friend. Rather, I had a little girl who simply didn't want her mother to leave. So my perspective flipped.

As we talked, Beth calmed down, and instead of yelling at anyone who passed by her, she expressed her sadness about my leaving. It became a sweet moment for the two of us. She still had to write an apology note to her siblings, but she was back in Green Brain. If I had let myself slip into Red Brain, I might have been attacking her behavior instead of addressing the root issue. She wasn't trying to be bad; she needed a listening ear and a hug. It was all about understanding the root of her behavior.

Investigate the Source

After everyone is safe and the fire is put out, it is often very important to know where and how the fire started, so that people can avoid having it happen in the same area again. The fire department will investigate to determine what the cause of the accident was or even if it was an accident. Sometimes a fire is caused by humans through intent or neglect. And even if the cause was a true accident, human mistakes or foolish actions may have assisted the fire's spread and endangered more lives. So the follow-up investigative work is almost as important as getting that fire doused to begin with.

It is important to identify where the Red Brain situation began and where the root issue is so we can address them and more wisely face them in the future. It's important not to be distracted by all the attention-grabbing flames we see on the outside, but to understand that the real issue is much more subtle, and often we have to dig through all the coals to find it. Part of a firefighter's job is to put out the fires once they start, but their job also includes educating others on fire awareness and prevention. If firefighters only put out flames but did not teach others about the danger of fires and how to prevent them, house fires would occur much more often, and there would be much more destruction.

It is the same with our children. It's important to bring them back into Green Brain, but we cannot stop there. We must also look deeper and address the real issue that brought them into Red Brain at the beginning.

Avoid Pouring Gas on the Fire
Stop, simplify, and redefine success—these are the main strategies to prevent escalating challenging situations into a full-on, chaotic Red Brain mode. But there are several everyday practices that your family can use to best avoid Red situations by staying in Green as much as possible.

Good Sleep
Being tired makes it easy to slip out of Green Brain; it greatly inhibits the ability to connect effectively. Tiredness also tends to trigger more behavioral issues in children. School-age children need at least ten hours of sleep per night, and if a child has difficulty getting out of bed in the morning, it is an indication that he or she may not be getting enough sleep.

Healthy Eating
A healthy diet keeps our body and brain in optimal condition. It is not simply about filling our own and our children's stomachs with foods such as pasta, potatoes, and rice, but about eating foods specifically nutritious for brain development such as fruits, vegetables, eggs, and meat. Healthy meals and snacks ensure concentration

and enhanced learning abilities. Children need regular nutrition every two to three hours to stay at an optimal functioning level.

My children always know that if they are hungry, there is a bowl of bananas in the kitchen for them to eat. If they don't want a banana and argue for ice cream instead, I know they're not really hungry.

Starting your child's day with a nutritional breakfast is important so that they arrive at school in Green Brain and make the best choices when you are not around. Though eating nutritional foods may be more costly, in the end, it can decrease illness, and it increases brain performance and learning abilities. The benefits certainly outweigh the costs compared to giving your children unhealthy, packaged snacks all the time.

Hydration

Any action or activity that redirects your focus, even for a moment, can help with self-regulation. When you need a quick break, take a drink of water. Keeping your body hydrated is essential to optimal performance and clear thinking. We seem to underestimate the importance of water, but dehydration seriously hinders children's abilities to learn.

Regular Exercise

The better our body feels, the better our brain works. Exercise is an excellent way to increase blood and oxygen flow to the brain, which increases the ability to learn and to make the right choices. It is also proven that positive behavior increases when exercising regularly.

Adapting Expectations

A disaster often happens when the expectations you have of your child do not match their developmental stage. When the expectation isn't met, it results in frustration, in which you, as the parent, are no longer working out of Green Brain. It could be that your children didn't finish their chores, or that they failed to be polite to a neighbor. In these moments, you often need to question whether this disaster was completely the child's fault, or did you as the parent somehow contribute? Was there something you could have done to prevent this? Children are going to be children, and the expectations you have for them need to fit their developmental stage.

If your two-year-old son is banging pots and pans in the kitchen, he is exploring his safe environment and learning how to create noise. He is not trying to be a bad child, going out of his way to create a mess for Mommy and Daddy; he knows no better. Your expectation of him can't be higher than what you've taught and trained him to know.

> Stop to listen, drop what you are doing, and roll with
> what your child needs.
> SHELLEY LEITH

Prepared for Battle

> Be on your guard; stand firm in the faith; be courageous;
> be strong.
> I CORINTHIANS 16:13, NIV

God calls us to be prepared for battle. And parenting is a sort of battle. So what does this preparation look like?

First, we need to know who the enemy is, who we are fighting. We are not in a battle with our children or our spouse. We are battling with spiritual forces that are all around us. We are battling temptation and our own irrational behavior.

Preparation for battle also means making sure your mind, soul, and body are ready for battle. Some traditions use the sign of the cross and say Father, Son, and Holy Spirit as they touch their head, stomach, and then shoulder to shoulder. I wondered what that meant, and I was told, "Lord I give You my mind, I give You my soul, and I give You my body." I found this to be a healthy ritual that helps me reflect on the meaning of the cross in a concrete way. I need to surrender and put everything at the foot of the cross.

As I say Father, Son, and Holy Spirit, I think of temptations. There are thoughts that are not from Him that I pay attention to or sometimes even embrace. I pray God will help my thoughts to be His thoughts.

I think of my soul. I need a spirit that is fresh and alive. I need living water that revitalizes my soul all through the day. I pray this phrase from Psalm 25:20: "Guard my soul, and deliver me!" I pray that He would protect me from evil.

I pray for my body. I ask God to help me to surrender temptations that are not healthy for my body. I need to eat the right kinds of food, exercise, and sleep so my body is in the best possible condition to serve.

Are we dressed for battle? Ephesians 6:10-11 says, "Finally, be strong in the Lord and in the strength of his might. Put on the whole armor of God, that you may be able to stand against the schemes of the devil."

We choose to turn again and again toward God, giving ourselves to Him, and He shields us with His mighty power to stand firm against the enemy and to be delivered from evil, that we may be freed to live into the fullness of life that He has for us. We cannot do any of this on our own!

I love the psalm that says. "Create in me a pure heart, O God, and renew a steadfast spirit within me" (Psalm 51:10, NIV). It talks about our spirit/soul. As parents, we are in a battle, yet sometimes we aren't even aware of it. Only as it sneaks up on us do we realize we aren't prepared for the battle. We need to be constantly equipped, not just when things are hard.

> Stand firm. Let nothing move you. Always give yourselves fully to the work of the Lord, because you know that your labor in the Lord is not in vain.

I CORINTHIANS 15:58, NIV

STOPLIGHT REFLECTIONS

1. In this chapter, we compared the struggle to stay in Green Brain and out of Red Brain to a firefighter battling flames. This fight is real, just as it would be for a solider fighting in a major battle. Read Ephesians 6:10-20. Think about what each part of the armor of God means in your life, in the context of parenting. How are you applying these protective and preventive measures? In what ways do you find that you are not able to be steadfast in your mind, soul, or body?

2. What are your priorities? Write out your daily schedule, including all the seemingly mundane little tasks. Examine what is taking up the majority of your time and energy. How much sleep do you get? How much time do you spend watching TV or scrolling through social media? How can this time be better spent connecting with your kids? How can you realign your schedule in order to better connect with your kids or have adequate time to rest? Think about sleep, food, exercise, and simplifying your family life.

3. We can't always prevent fires from starting, but we can put them out before they grow out of control. We need to be aware that something isn't right before the fire really gets roaring. Catch it in Yellow before it flares up into Red.

What are some ways you are stopping fires from growing in your home?

Prayer

God, You are my shepherd; You give me everything I need! When I am exhausted, You make me lie down in green pastures. When I am empty of resources, You lead me beside still waters. When I feel that my patience is in tatters, You restore my soul. Good Shepherd, be in me. Be my patience, my wisdom, my comfort, and my good humor! Fill me daily with Yourself, Shepherd of my Soul.

CHAPTER 7

Parenting in Relationship: Boundaries and Connection

JOSEPH WAS LYING ON THE COUCH, taking up all of the seats. I came in to sit down. "Joseph, can you move over, please?"

What a concept: Mom wanting to sit down. Instead of moving over, though, he let out a clearly annoyed sigh, got up, and stormed out of the room.

"What was that about?" I said indignantly to my husband, feeling hurt by my son. My emotions were rising. I was in Yellow, well on my way to Red as I questioned my son's love for his own mother. *He can't disrespect me like that. He is going to have to explain himself, and it better be good!*

As I started to march out of the room, now fully in Red Brain, to go deal with my teenager, my husband stopped me. "Are you going in there in Red Brain?" he said. *Are you really able to make him feel safe and connected with you right now?*

I stopped. My husband caught me neglecting my own parenting philosophy!

"You both are unsafe right now and going there to scold him is not going to solve anything," he said.

And he was right.

The Stoplight Approach to Discipline

As we looked at earlier in this book, many of us parent our children the way we were parented. Growing up, we observed and experienced how our parents interacted with us, how they loved us, how they provided and cared for us—and how they disciplined and punished us. (That's one we always remember, for some reason.) These areas of parenting become ingrained in how we parent our own children.

My mom and dad parented me in a fashion similar to the way they were parented, and I am prone to continue that pattern when dealing with my own children. So when my son got upset and stormed off, my instincts—based on how I had been raised—were to immediately address the disrespectful behavior of my teenager. My focus was on what had happened (past behavior) and how I could control him. Thankfully, my husband stopped me and helped me remember that as a Stoplight parent, I want my focus to be on the future.

My son needs to learn to be respectful, of course. But as we've been discovering in our examination of God's design in the human brain, this area of parenting happens best in the context of relationship. By marching into his room in Red Brain and demanding that he respect his mother, I am threatening that relationship. If he's not already in a Red state, he is likely to mirror my Red state, and any opportunity to learn will be drastically reduced. And my ability to coach him will also be significantly reduced. Remember, we only use around fifty percent of our IQ while in a Red state.

It's in these Red-brain times that we must remember the very important difference between punishment and discipline. These two words are often used as synonyms, but the distinction between these words can mean the difference between a calm Green home and an unsafe Red home.

Discipline is not punishment. Using punishment as discipline is like using chili peppers instead of using bell peppers for cooking a meal. They seem similar at a glance, but how you use and prepare each is very different. (Not to mention the level of heat will vary in the final meal.) In the same way, the effects that punishment and discipline have on a child's brain differ vastly.

Punishment concerns itself with the past. Punishing means putting and often keeping our children in Yellow or Red Brain for the duration of whatever punishment we feel is appropriate for the past misbehavior. Punishment causes children to feel unsafe and pushed away from the love they are designed to feel from their parents. Moreover, because children are in Yellow and Red Brain during this time, they are unable to learn well from their mistakes. They obey out of fear and not a change of heart.

Discipline is focused on the future. Above all, it means helping our kids understand in their heart how making better choices create better outcomes. Discipline is about learning.

Who Is God?

Growing up, I often thought of God as an angry, unapproachable, and judgmental God, and I could never do right in His eyes. And I thought of Jesus as the kind and loving friend, a mediator between the fearsome Father and me. Needless to say, I didn't have a complete understanding of the Trinity.

As I studied the basics of brain science behind the Stoplight Approach, I've been awakened to a whole new image of who God is and how He has created us for relationship. The kind, loving

Jesus is still God. And Jesus says, "Whoever has seen me has seen the Father" (John 14:9).

My perspective of God had been focused on fear and shame rather than on the relationship that He desires with me. But He's helped me understand that He would never want me to fear Him, because that would prevent me from getting close to Him. How could we build a relationship if I never tried to be close to Him? I now recognize that I am invited into a relationship with the Trinity.

My understanding of God has also changed the way I view my kids, and I've had to continually re-evaluate the aspects of my parenting that have involved fear and shame. I can think of many times where I used fear-based statements on my kids: "Wait until your dad gets home!" or "You're in such big trouble!" Why did I say these things? Why do I want my children to *fear* their own mother? Does God want me to fear Him in a way that drops my brain in a state of Red? As I re-evaluate my image of God, I've had to continually re-evaluate the aspects of my parenting that have involved fear and shame.

The Unwanted Effects of Punishment and Rewards

At two years of age, Catherine was strong-willed. Tired and pregnant with my second child, I was frustrated. I only wanted to do what was best for her—to protect her and help her make good decisions. So I swatted her on the bottom when I caught her misbehaving.

Apparently, Catherine had a very high pain tolerance. She would later continue the behavior that I'd caught her doing. So I spanked her again. Still, she continued. *What is wrong with this child?* I thought.

But then I stopped. *What was I doing? I am a professor, for goodness sake!* Surely if I can have control in a classroom, I can—and need to—use some similar skills in my own home.

At the time, I was just beginning to understand that crucial distinction between punishment and discipline. Parents often notice that punishment tends to produce quick results: Our children listen and obey quite nicely when we inflict, or threaten to inflict, some form of pain. We may even get a sense of gratification when see that such consequences can control our kids' behavior.

But a constant fear-based system of punishing misbehavior shifts a child repeatedly into Red Brain, where they begin to feel unsafe. Again, when in Red Brain, a child's ability to learn is actually diminished, and the relationship with their parent is threatened. This can have dramatic implications in the future. If the relationship between parents and a child is compromised, the child will be less likely to see parents as the people to go to when he or she is hurt or afraid. So when kids mess up, which they will, instead of seeking out a parent's help to correct the situation, their instinct will be to cover up or hide the issue.

Remember, we want to reduce the amount of time our children are in Red or Yellow Brain. While the chemicals released by the brain in these states are useful for dealing with dangerous or stressful situations, prolonged exposure is not healthy for a growing brain.

Many parents use a system of rewards for good behavior. While rewards can be used well in some circumstances—perhaps as motivation for chores or schoolwork—and they do not have the same downside of flipping a child to Yellow or Red, they are not a good way to teach positive behaviors and values. The reason is that rewards tend to lose their effectiveness, and parents end up having to promise greater and greater rewards in order to compel the desired behavior. When the reward loses its attraction, a child often reverts to behaving in whatever way they want because their motivation for "good" behavior was really just for the promise of a reward, for reasons *outside* of themselves.

Remember that children are imitators. They will learn to interact with others from how you interact with them. If rewards and punishment are how you get compliance, these are the tools your kids will learn are the most effective way to deal with life. They may start to see friendships and relationships in a purely transactional way.

Consider the value of sharing toys or other possessions. If a child learns to share because they will get a reward, they learn to view other relationships in terms of what they will get out of them. If they learn to share because sharing itself is valued in your family, and they are taught to notice that their actions have positive effects on others, they begin to internalize these values. If you model empathy with firm boundaries, they will learn to relate with understanding while setting limits to behavior—all in the context of a healthy relationship.

Relationship-Based Discipline

To be truly effective, parenting must happen in the context of relationship, in a home where children feel safe, loved, and valued. Discipline requires love, patience, wisdom, time, and effort, which means we need to be in Green Brain a lot more of the time than we are in Red Brain.

First, we must be able to recognize which brain state both our kids and we as parents are operating in. Being in Green Brain means we can use most of our brain to relate to our child and think calmly and critically about a situation. In turn, our children need to be in Green so that they are able to learn and understand how to change their behavior for the next time. If they are not in Green, our first goal is to help them feel safe, loved, and valued.

We need to be a sort of detective to see the needs behind a child's behavior and misbehavior. Dr. Ross Greene, a modern pioneer in the area of working with kids who have behavior challenges, has observed that many behavioral challenges are rooted at a much lower level than what parents might interpret in the heat of the moment. It may not be defiance or a bad attitude. Greene suggests that we first ask ourselves the question, "What are my child's unmet needs, unsolved problems, or lack of skills?" Unmet needs must be addressed first before a child has the capacity to focus on unsolved problems and learning skills.[1]

Once in Green, new skills, values, and appropriate behaviors are taught and practiced. Instead of focusing on external motivators like rewards and punishments, most of your attention should be on coaching your child using internal motivators as your son or daughter develops a moral identity in line with family values.

Even though I've done my fair share of brain science research, I can still find myself falling back into fear-based parenting when I go into Yellow or Red. I know all of the reasons why I shouldn't yell at my child and send them to their room, but when I'm in Red Brain, I want to feel like I'm back in control of the situation. I suppose many parents can relate: It's a perceived loss of control that sends us spiraling toward Red to begin with.

So in those moments, I don't feel like putting in the effort to calmly and wisely discipline my child. When kids tell me how much they hate me, I want them to pay for how they hurt me! But lately, I've been practicing a question similar to what Dr. Greene recommends: I ask myself if the child is safe or unsafe.

If I can control myself enough to ask this question, I'm able to start looking at the child instead of the situation. Yes, the child has disobeyed or disrespected me, but she is unsafe, in Yellow or Red Brain, and therefore I need to draw her close before trying to discipline and train her. I still fail at points, but through practice, I am seeing how beneficial and rewarding this approach is to parenting, both for myself and for my children.

As parents, we speak through our tone of voice and body language more than we think. Kids can pick up on these signals, even if we use the "right words" when responding to their misbehavior. So get yourself to Green first.

Think back to a recent interaction you had with your child and evaluate whether your words, body language, or tone of voice in any way communicated shame, lack of value, or criticism. Was your tone of voice demeaning? Did your cell phone distract you, communicating a lack of worth to the child? Did you respond sarcastically?

According to Dr. Albert Mehrabian of UCLA, your tone of voice makes up about 38% of what you communicate to someone. So whether you are joking, yelling, whispering, or speaking sarcastically, your tone by itself can create shame in a child. What's more, 55% of what you communicate is entirely nonverbal. So the way we physically present ourselves to our children is a big factor in their emotional safety. A shake of the head, rolling of our eyes, an angry face, throwing our arms in the air, ignoring their presence, putting our head in our hands, avoiding eye contact, giving attention to our cell phones more than our children—these things can all produce shame in our children.[2]

Once all of our communication is sending the same message to the child—whether safety, value, or love—then we have a chance to make a lasting difference in coaching and teaching our kids. Continue reflecting Green: Keep your face calm, bend down to below the child's eye level, use few words, give eye contact, smile, don't react immediately, practice active listening, ask questions, put away your cell phone, bring your child close, unfold your arms, use positive touch.

Then ask yourself, "Would I speak in this tone to an adult?" Your goal is to maintain the safe environment that allows your child to learn and grow.

Thinking through potential misbehavior ahead of time and deciding which of the following actions would be most suitable to use will help greatly. By anticipating potential problems and planning our responses ahead of time, we will be more able to stay in

If we want our homes to be Green, we need to have conversations that are Green as well.

Red: volatile, shut down, yelling

Yellow: distracted, disconnected, stressed

Green: present, listening, finding solutions

Watch **what** you say, **how** you say it, and **when** you say it.

Green Brain ourselves, helping to create the Green home environment we desire to have. Life isn't always that simple, though, and you will have moments when you flip to Red, as will your children. In the next chapter, we will look at the best way to move forward when someone has flipped to Red.

It is important to stress that I am not promoting a weak, permissive approach to parenting. Children need boundaries and rules to learn what is positive and what is negative behavior. Rather, the

Stoplight Approach gives us a lens through which to understand the science of the brain and the value of relationships to help us to raise our children to become emotionally intelligent and socially responsible adults.

Taking Care of the Flock

We've all heard various interpretations of the corporal punishment language found in Proverbs 13:24—the "spare the rod, spoil the child" axiom. Given the context of the original writing, this proverb is best understood as a comparison between parenting and a shepherd looking after sheep. In the time and place that verse was written, shepherding was a common job, and most people had a basic understanding of how it worked.

To take care of his flock of sheep, a shepherd used a crook—a long, sturdy stick with a hook on one end. The hook end is used for pulling sheep out of holes they've fallen into or away from dangers. The rod was used to guide the sheep, tapping the ground or the sheep to keep them on the right path when they try to wander away. The rod probably felt unpleasant when the shepherd needed to use it on a sheep, but it provided structure and boundaries, ensuring that sheep didn't get lost. A shepherd would also use his rod to protect the flock from wild animals.

I like to think of the rod from the sheep's perspective. The rod guides him safely along their travels, keeping him from external harm. In some small way, the sheep recognizes that the shepherd means safety, that he always has his rod and can skillfully use it, when necessary, to correct the flock's path and protect the sheep from danger.

With an understanding of what *rod* means, we can better understand the "Whoever spares the rod hates their children" wording (NIV). The author is saying that the one who doesn't provide guidance, teaching, and protection (the things that a rod provides for sheep) for their child is reasonably described as hating the child. The parent is simply not parenting well.

We can see this in the world around us too; most children who don't have supportive, guiding parents struggle significantly in school, in relationships, and in the workplace.

Now take a look at the second half of the verse, which mirrors the first, "but the one who loves their children is careful to discipline them." Discipline means to teach, guide, and give consequences. It comes from the same root word as *disciple*. Here, the reverse situation is presented: the parent who does give their child teaching and guidance loves their child.

Loving parents guide their children back to the right path when they've strayed.

Remember that fear must not be the foundation of this relationship. A person is fearful when they are in Red Brain, so a loving parent-child relationship avoids putting the other person in Red. When dealing with a child's misbehavior, loving parents remain in Green, using their language and their love to guide children through connection and correction rather than fear-based punishment.

Consider God's heart for His children: "I am the good shepherd. I know my own and my own know me, just as the Father knows me and I know the Father; and I lay down my life for the sheep" (John 10:14-15). He loves us, knows us—all of our weaknesses—and loves us even to the laying down of His life for us. He is the Good Shepherd!

Of course, none of us can meet the perfect standard of Jesus. We all mess up. During those times, we need to ask God's forgiveness and then, with His help, plan how to do better next time. Parents are in the process of learning, growing, and developing into better people, just as their children are. We look to our loving Father for His support and guidance in this process.

STOPLIGHT REFLECTIONS

1. Think back to a situation in which your child misbehaved. Did your perceptions of the event and your resulting feelings reflect a focus on discipline or punishment? What was going on "below the surface" in that situation? If you could go back to that event, what would you change?

2. Think about a time from your own childhood when you were punished for a negative behavior. Did you feel the punishment helped you learn to behave better, or did it cause you to feel shame? Why or why not?

3. How does your view of God impact the way you parent your child? What do you see when you imagine His face? Is He an angry judge waiting to punish you?

4. To explore the goodness of God, our Shepherd, read Psalm 23 slowly aloud. Notice that there is nothing for the sheep to fear from the Shepherd. Let His goodness and mercy follow you as you shepherd your own children.

Prayer

Thank You, God, that You never shame me. Rather, You took my shame upon Yourself on the cross. I am overcome by Your deep love and respect for me as Your child and image-bearer. Help me to see and respect Your beautiful image in each of my children. Give me Your wisdom and patience to lead them as You lead me.

CHAPTER 8

Mending Your Mess-ups: Repairing Relationships

My daughter had an incident on the soccer field in which she was quite disrespectful to her coach. The coach was understandably frustrated and told my daughter that she had lost the privilege of playing in the next game. We sat down with her and discussed how the coach felt. The coach was in Red Brain in relation to our daughter, feeling unsafe around her, so our daughter needed to rebuild the relationship with her coach before they could have success together.

Our daughter agreed that she needed to repair the relationship, so she sat down to write a very thoughtful apology note, asking for forgiveness and stating what she had done wrong. These words would allow her coach to move from Red to Yellow and feel safe again with her as part of the team. Then our daughter told her coach that she really did value her and all of the work she did, helping the coach now move from Yellow to Green.

Finally, out daughter addressed how her behavior would be different in the future. Now in Green herself, she was showing her coach how she could problem-solve to prevent the behavior from being an ongoing issue. She came up with a solution, and they agreed on a compromise that allowed her to play on the team. Our daughter understood the consequences if she was disrespectful again.

Repairing relationships is rarely easy. When we go into Red, we can be harmful to those around us. We say and do things we later regret, and our relationships are ruptured, whether it be with our spouse, friend, or child.

Reconnection after a Disconnection

Yes, sometimes we freak out, as our daughter did during the heat of a soccer competition. Red Brain reactions (and overreactions) happen. They happen to kids, and they happen to parents.

Parents, you can probably recognize that when you are in Red Brain, you are not capable of connecting emotionally with your child. If this type of reaction is continued and prolonged, it can be very confusing and even harmful to your child. Approaching your children after a Red Brain moment—apologizing and explaining the situation—helps them create a healthy, more accurate narrative about the event in which they can avoid internalizing the experience as being their fault.

So don't run away after you've calmed down. Process the event together. Apologize and explain. "Hey, kiddo, Daddy just went into Red Brain and did not make the right choice. I am sorry. Can you forgive me?"

It may be difficult, but it's so important to pursue reconnection after a disconnection. Modeling of healthy relationships for your child will enhance their ability to nurture meaningful relationships in the future.

When We Hurt

Forgiveness has often been a struggle for me. I give myself excuses for the hurt I feel that was caused by other people's actions. When I'm in Yellow—when I'm stressed, tired, and not as focused— I may hurt others as I'm less aware of their feelings in those moments. When I'm in Red, I say things out loud because I'm angry. In Red, my thoughts and words are much more destructive. Red is not healthy, but my experience in that state has at least helped me understand a little about the words of Jesus as He hung on the cross: "Father, forgive them, for they know not what they do" (Luke 23:34). In Red, we do not really know what we are doing.

When my family hurts me, it's easy to internalize that shame and hurt. *If I were a better mom, this wouldn't have happened.*

I was once wisely told that if I get hurt, I had to focus first on forgiving instead of searching for a way to absorb the fault. It's true: When people hurt us, forgiveness is the answer! Holding on to the pain and the shame and the guilt hurts you far more than it hurts anyone else.

When my children are in Yellow or Red, they say and do mean things. I have to forgive them, for they often do not realize what they are doing and how it is hurting me. And when I don't acknowledge the hurt my child has caused me, I end up resenting my child, creating an invisible barrier between myself and them. Over time, this hurt can accumulate—as more and more hurt is inflicted, that barrier can grow larger and larger.

Letting go of the pain, resentment, and resulting guilt has been one of my most difficult parenting journeys. It's not about your children coming to you and asking for forgiveness; you have to take it to the foot of the Cross. Forgiveness is the essence of the gospel—Jesus giving us His sacrificial love in the context of forgiveness! When I forgive, I am able to look at my children with love—the way God sees them, and the way God sees me. It is a humbling experience!

Fix It, Treasure It, Change It

Many parents never create a resolution for the future after they react in Red Brain, and this can be very damaging to the effort of trying to live more in Green. When you take responsibility for your actions, you are modeling this behavior for your children, who will then take responsibility for their actions in relationships with others. Let's look at the way we want to model healthy reconnection after disconnection.

Dr. Dan Siegel uses three words to help parents model healthy reconnection after disconnection: repair, reconnect, and re-evaluate. Repair and reconnect with your child when either of you has gone into Red and the relationship has been ruptured. Then re-evaluate the situation so that you can look at what went wrong and find strategies to avoid the same incident happening again.[1]

Repair Needs Forgiveness

When we have created a rupture in a relationship, we have gone into Red. Now we need to fix it. You have disconnected with your child—now it's important to repair the relationship, and that requires forgiveness. It can be very difficult to ask for forgiveness from a child, but it is crucial to create healthy relationships. Sometimes we as parents don't apologize because of our own pride, or we feel defensive because we believe the child deserved our anger. So instead of justifying your behavior, say to your child, "I was wrong to yell at you even though I didn't like what you were doing. I should never yell at you like that. Will you forgive me?" We know that when someone is in Red, they are very unsafe, so when we say sorry, it's the beginning of the process of reconciliation and ultimately rebuilding the relationship. Seeking forgiveness is not conditional on the other person changing their behavior. Saying "I'm sorry" is not a check mark on a to-do list. Truly asking for forgiveness takes away the anger and bitterness inside ourselves and opens the door to reconnecting and reestablishing relationships.

Children need to work through these same steps. A child who flipped to Red may need to repair relationships with parents, siblings, friends, or all of the above. To truly mean "I'm sorry," the child will need to be back to Green. In some situations, a verbal apology is sufficient, but often a written note is more effective.

Reconnection Needs Value

The second step is reconnection. Through reconnection, the parent values the child, showing them how important they are to the parent. We often want to skip step one and move directly to step two, but if reconnection happens without repair first, then ruptures will be pushed under the carpet, and the result is insecure relationships. Reconnection is showing someone that you care about your relationship with them, that you treasure it. Tell them why they are important to you. You have common ground, things you both care about that make you care about each other. Let them know what connects you together and why you want to stay connected. The worst thing you can do is pretend that nothing happened and try to move on as if the relationship is fine. The result is broken trust.

When children practice reconnection, it might be something simple, like giving a sibling a hug. If they are writing an apology note, it might include reconnection in the form of a compliment. Brainstorm with your child. If they are still learning the skill of reconnection, perhaps they offer to play a game of the other's choice, or do their after-dinner chores, or put the Lego creation back together.

Re-evaluation Needs Strategies

Repair and reconnection are vital, but they are incomplete without re-evaluation. Re-evaluation is the final step, creating strategies to help avoid ruptures in the future. This step uses problem-solving skills to figure out how you will change for next time. If the step of re-evaluation is not taken after reconnection, then no change will happen; the love and value are conditional because no plan is put in place to change future behavior. The important aspect of re-evaluation is that the person who went to Red is attempting to change and attempting to communicate that desire to the other person. The expectation is not that we never go to Red, but that when we do, we try to be proactive, so that next time, in a similar circumstance, we are less likely to do so. Be patient with yourself and your children if the strategy isn't successful and you, or they, need to work through this process again—and again.

Learning to repair, reconnect, and re-evaluate is a life skill that will help your children have healthy relationships. We can model and teach them that when there is a relationship rupture, we need to fix it, treasure it, and change it for next time.

> Children do not need perfect parents; they need
> repentant parents.
> PHILLIP MAMALAKIS

Bad Moms

So many days I've felt like a failure. At the end of every day, lying awake, I would make a list of all the things I did wrong. Anything I did right felt irrelevant. Thinking about my long list of wrongs, I thought I had failed as a mom. I was not a perfect parent. I could give you a sample of my list: My house was a mess. My kids weren't getting along. I yelled at my kids. I would compare myself to other moms who seemed to have it all together!

Have you ever thought about whose standards you are trying to measure up to? Why do I always wind up feeling like garbage?

One day, I started to analyze my list. What is this unattainable list that I measure myself against? Is it God's list? Does God hold up a list each day and write *Failed* with a big red X across it? Does He glare down upon us with shame and disappointment? Is this list that I compare myself to one that I created in His name, thinking it was what He wanted from us? If it is a standard that condemns me to shame and guilt that has made me feel so bad, then it is not from God! How does God look at me? I can't be perfect, because only He is. I am human. I make mistakes. I need to own those mistakes and ask for forgiveness!

Children do not need perfect parents, but they do need repentant parents. I have to let go of the guilt that I carry. I have to come to the foot of the Cross and lay out my burden of guilt—a burden I was never meant to carry—knowing that because of the Cross, Jesus will give me the ability to parent my children in the way that He wants.

Power in Forgiveness

Forgive us our debts, as we also have forgiven our debtors.
MATTHEW 6:12

God intends for our home to be a sanctuary, a safe place for all who live there and for all who enter. It doesn't have perfect people in it, but in God's grace it is filled with people who are rooted and grounded in the generous love, goodness, and tenderness of God. He is a sanctuary for us; we learn that we are safe in His presence. He knows we cannot parent our children perfectly!

When we have wronged our children or betrayed their trust, God is a safe refuge for us; He waits for us to come to Him for forgiveness. With His help, we can turn to those whom we have wounded. We humbly ask our children to forgive us for what we have done or said.

Each time we ask for forgiveness, we are not simply "making things right again," but we are giving God the opportunity to create something new, an invitation to "Create in me a clean heart" (Psalm 51:10). We are giving God the opportunity to restore our children's shredded dignity and wounded spirits, freeing them to become healthier, stronger human beings. Our home is restored as a sanctuary in which each person can explore, create, and grow into who God has uniquely made them to be.

Our lives can be very messy! We all need God's help to repair our relationships when they need mending. And repentance is one of God's greatest gifts to us. It is not about guilt and fear; it is about turning away from our sinful action, turning our face to God, asking for His forgiveness, and inviting the living waters of Christ to flow through us, renewing us with His very life. It is the heart of the gospel, and the heart of what it means to live in God's Kingdom.

STOPLIGHT REFLECTIONS

1. At the core of the Christian faith is love and forgiveness. As we look at the significance of the Cross and how Jesus forgave us (without our doing anything to deserve it), how does that impact our parenting?

2. Is confession and forgiveness part of your daily practice? In the coming weeks, practice a heart of gratitude for what you treasure about your family, and repentance for the things you've done wrongly. Talk to each person in your family and say one thing you're thankful for, one thing you did today that you need forgiveness for, and one request from God.

Prayer

God, I love You and thank You. When I mess up, You wait for me to turn to You. Forgive me for when I have been more concerned with myself rather than others. Forgive me for holding grudges. Forgive me for my indifference to You. I praise You that You show mercy! I bask in the joy of Your forgiveness. Create in me a new spirit!

CHAPTER 9

Roots of Misbehavior: Looking Deeper

IT WAS SIX THIRTY on a Saturday morning. My husband was away, so I knew I was on duty, but I was looking forward to sleeping in until at least seven thirty. All the kids know the rules: *Don't wake Mommy up in the morning.*

My kids knew that if they woke up before seven thirty, well, that was what the stack of books beside their bed was for. So why did the shrieks of children come wafting up to my window, at six thirty, from the backyard? I heard the van door slam, accompanied by more squeals. Immediately, I conjured up the image of squashed fingers. My heart raced. I was in Red, scared by the worst-case scenario which my imagination presented me, and very angry that I was now up and out of bed at 6:33 on a Saturday morning. I stomped downstairs, one very unhappy mama. Thankfully, by the time I got to the bottom of the stairs, I remembered, "Stoplight starts with you," and I took a deep breath. In those moments, I heard the giggle of a child at play, and I realized the shrieks and squeals that woke me had been happy ones. I stepped out into the morning sun. Careful to keep my tone neutral, I called, "Peter, David, Benjamin, come here." Three little boys came running from different directions. "What are you doing?" I asked casually.

"Playing hide-and-seek!" Peter answered enthusiastically.

"Oh! And what are you supposed to be doing in the morning before mommy wakes up?"

Slowly the wheels turned, and realization hit them, "Stay in bed and read books."

I nodded. "It is time for a redo. Back to your beds and your books. You can finish your game after breakfast, but I'm going to need you to give me a little extra sleep-in time since I had to get up early just now. I'll see you all at 7:45. Books and quiet until then—got it?" Reluctantly, they shuffled back to bed, while I, anything but reluctant, snuggled back under my covers for a few more precious minutes of sleep.

The Roots of Misbehavior

Have you ever assumed the worst about somebody and then quickly regretted jumping to those conclusions? As parents, we often see some behavior or another and jump to conclusions, thinking we understand the motivation of the behavior. Sometimes kids are firmly in Green Brain, but their impulsive, thoughtless actions seem very Red. Other times the Red behavior comes from a defiant or angry attitude because they most definitely are in Red. Once again, being a parent means being a detective. It means we need to stop what we are doing—no parenting from the sidelines—and focus on the child.

Look at their behaviors, their body language, and their tone of voice to determine what is really going on. The morning when

I woke to what appeared to be a Red situation—children outside unsupervised, fingers in danger of being slammed in house and car doors, rules being disobeyed—my "What are you doing?" question was not an idle one. I needed to know where they were at. The kids' answers gave insight into what brain state they were in as well as the root and motivation of their behavior. Had the answers been, "David hit me, so . . ." and "But Peter took my book first. . . ." I would have known we were dealing with Yellow- or Red-rooted behavior, and my response would have been different. Their happy answer of "Playing hide-and-seek" cued me immediately into the fact that they were all in Green Brain, and this was a Green-rooted misbehavior.

What appears to be the same behavior can come from three different brain states. In Green Brain, rough play means we respond with coaching, because our kids have the capacity to learn in those moments. In Yellow Brain, an impatient squabble means we respond with reconnecting with our children. In Red Brain, an angry fight would mean our first priority is to calm the kids down and start moving them to Green.

To effectively parent in these mixed-message situations, parents need to discover the brain state of the child so they can address it in an appropriate manner.

In Green, we are able to learn, so our response to Green-rooted behavior is teaching, training, and helping kids learn skills. Green roots need coaching. The vast majority of parenting is spent dealing with Green-rooted behavior. Children live in the moment. They are thoughtless and impulsive. Since their frontal cortex is not fully developed until they are in their twenties, young people don't always think ahead. They need practice, a chance to learn, and a coach to help them do that.

When a child is in Yellow, they are often feeling stressed, anxious, undervalued, and unloved. They need to know they matter.

Yellow-rooted behavior requires connection. We pull our child close (literally or figuratively) to show them we care. Then we try to determine their unmet needs, unsolved problems, or undeveloped skills. Their emotional brain is filtering everything, and they are using only about 75% of their IQ ability. When misbehavior has Yellow roots, we can help them process and move forward by limiting options to two choices.

Red-rooted behavior is unsafe. The child is unsafe to themselves and perhaps to others around them. Red-rooted behavior needs calming. When behavior is rooted in Red, the parent's focus should be on the child, not the behavior.

When misbehavior has Green roots, we teach, train, and coach a child how to change that behavior. When misbehavior has Yellow roots, our focus is on connection with the child, but we also come alongside our child to redirect and correct misbehavior together. And, of course, Red means stop. When the roots of misbehavior are Red, we stop thinking about the behavior and all our focus is on helping the child be safe and get back to Green.

Again, in order for us as parents to have a Green response to misbehavior, we need to get ourselves to Green first. Take a few moments to breathe deeply or grab a glass of water so you are ready to look beyond the behavior and see the child.

Where's the Instruction Manual?

Sometimes God puts us in stressful situations in order to help us grow. Maybe He gives us different kinds of children with different personalities and different struggles. And, of course, none of our children arrive with an instruction manual. We need to parent our children as unique individuals, being careful that we don't treat each child the same.

The Stoplight Approach is rarely a formula—we have to apply what we've learned with thought and care. When I hear my daughters fighting upstairs, I don't know if their behavior is rooted in Red, Yellow, or Green. How I deal with each of my daughters is going to be different, because each could be in a different brain state at the time. And that's before considering their very different personalities and the environment in which they have lived. Just like two kids on a soccer team will be coached differently, each of my kids will need to be coached and trained differently.

What's more, my home is constantly changing over time! My oldest daughter grew up with six younger children at home, while my youngest is growing up with a completely different dynamic. What worked with one kid won't always work with the others. I am also growing as a person—I'm not the same person I was when I had my first child. God is calling me to look at my children through His eyes—not just the eyes of brain science. I need God's wisdom—not just knowledge about how my children's brains work.

Proactive Parenting

A huge part of parenting is in prevention. As previously discussed, getting enough sleep, food, and exercise play an important role in a child's ability to remain in Green. Before we dig deeper into handling Red or Yellow behavior, we are going to look at three key components of being a safe and proactive parent for your children: routine, supervision, and rules.

Routine. Every child needs clearly understood structure and routine. This ordinary consistency is a powerful way to decrease behavioral issues because it makes the child's world feel safe and predictable. It takes away the need for unexpected demands on the child. Daily routines are just a part of life—brushing teeth before bed, washing hands before eating, story time before bed. If your child isn't getting his homework completed every day, set out a scheduled time in his daily routine in which he can complete it. This way, both you and your child know the expectations and desired outcome.

Getting ready for bed has often been a big ordeal in my house. Some of my kids can stop what they are doing immediately and get ready for bed without any fuss, while my other kids simply cannot respond that quickly, even if they are in Green Brain. They need at least ten minutes to process and understand the expectations on them and to finish up their activities before switching into bedtime routines. Otherwise, they flip into Red, and nobody is happy. An evening routine helps this transition go smoother.

Yet flexibility is also important. In my family, there are days when we stay on schedule, days when we try to stay on schedule, and days we throw the schedule out the window just as the day is getting started.

Life happens, and you shouldn't feel guilty about that. If we kept to our schedule perfectly every day, I can't imagine all of the amazing life experiences my children would have missed out on! When we are in Yellow or Red Brain, we can easily become rigid in our routines and rules, but this can tear down relationships. Make routines a part of family life, but don't throw away every chance to be spontaneous!

More Guidance. Often children misbehave because they need an adult to give them new ideas or some choices for wise behavior. And there are often warning signs at the beginning of a downward spiral. By staying tuned in to our kids, an intervention in this process is possible and is much easier to deal with than the bottom of the spiral—the bad behavior. Simply spending more time being in the same room as your child can reduce many issues.

My teen son has told us that what he has loved about our parenting is that he was always invited into various projects growing up. Looking back, we see this has been a pattern of our parenting. We just spend lots of time with our kids, allowing them to "help out" with our daily activities, and it has made them feel loved, valued, and appreciated because we intentionally include them.

Clear Expectations. One good method of setting rules is to have your children help create them during the beginning of a change, such as the new school year, the summer break, or a move. This ensures that everyone knows, understands, and agrees upon the expectations.

If you are not the one to establish the structure and rules of your home, your children will be quick to structure it for you— and not necessarily in the way you would like. Our rules need to be simple and achievable, but they also need to be flexible depending on the needs of the child or the circumstances of the day or week. These should be practiced and rehearsed while in Green Brain so that when they need to be reinforced, the child already knows the expectations. Posting these rules in your house in a positive, eye-catching way will help your children to follow them. When children clearly recognize what is expected of them, they are more likely to obey because they are more intrinsically motivated to do what is right according to the standards you have discussed together. Kids begin to see the principles behind the rules, particularly as they grow older, encouraging them to take responsibility and to use those morals as a compass for their lives. They begin to understand the "why" behind every rule.

One effective way to frame rules is in terms of a family mission statement. Here is ours:

> We are a loving, caring, sharing family. We are a family of grace that protects each other's weaknesses and celebrates each other's strengths. We have an attitude of service.
>
> ORR FAMILY MISSION STATEMENT

Our family built our mission statement many years ago when the kids were young. As they have grown older, we've tweaked the statement, adding sentences that reflect the kind of family we strive to be. Of course, I know we have not always been loving, caring, and sharing, but we always return to our goal. When someone is not making the right choice, if we are in a hard situation, or if someone is upset, we can always ask ourselves, "What kind of family are we?" and we remember our actions need to reflect loving, caring, and sharing. Our desire to show an attitude of service calls us to reach out to others in a way that reflects the values captured in our mission statement. No easy task, but much easier in a family that tries its best to be in Green!

"See that...it says I'm the boss of all the toys."

It is important to remember that there are always exceptions to the rules. Maybe your teenager's bedtime is at ten o'clock, but you are watching a movie together. The rule says they need to go to bed, but this is a bonding time between parent and child. Structure is good, but there are times when exceptions are needed. We, as parents, can become so focused on rules that we forget about the relationships.

Not long ago, my parents came to visit. The plane was arriving late at night, past the kids' bedtime, and it was a school night. Of course, our normal rules would have kept the kids home to go to bed on time, and then see Granny and Papa in the morning. But we made an exception. My kids hadn't seen their grandparents in over a year, and they were ecstatic about the visit. I knew I would have to deal with tired kids the next day, but the relationship between my parents and their grandchildren was more important in that moment.

Growing in Green

My eldest daughter's thoughts on our family mission statement:

When I was 10, my sister, who was adopted first, came into our home. She moved into my room, and she was a terror! That was hard. It's been hard to love all of my siblings all of the time.

We have a family mission statement. My parents have taught this to me since I learned to talk. It has helped all of us in being a loving family.

The first line is, "We are a loving, caring, sharing family." Even my youngest brother knows this line. If the little ones are not getting along, my mother says, "What kind of family are we?" My brother can understand this question and can understand what being a loving, caring, sharing family means.

The second line is, "We're a family of grace." It means we protect each other in our weaknesses and encourage each other in our strengths. If we're fighting about who's better or more deserving, we're reminded of this line. My younger sisters are getting to know this part.

The third line is, "We're a family of service." To me, this means we're available to help others. We want to be a family that is open. We want to have an attitude of giving. We want to think about what we can do for others, not what we want for ourselves. All of these statements are what my family strives to be.

Power of Words

> Do not provoke your children to anger, but bring them up in the discipline and instruction of the Lord.
>
> EPHESIANS 6:4

Our words are powerful! They can give joy and healing to our children. Or they can wound their spirit. How many times have we wished we could take our words back or wished we could have paused for a moment to seek God's help in seeing our children as He sees them?

It was midday in Samaria, and the sun was merciless. Jesus, tired and thirsty, sat down on the edge of the well to rest for a while. Most Jews would have bypassed the town on their travels, for they despised the people of Samaria. A Samaritan woman, rejected even by her own people, approached with her water jar. When Jesus saw her, He knew who she was. He knew her sin— that she had lived with six men, and He also knew the depth of her brokenness.

Jesus spoke first and asked her to draw water and give Him a drink. The woman was astonished. There wasn't a hint of disdain or rejection in the man's voice! Curious, she asked a question. "How is it that you, a Jew, ask for a drink from me, a woman of Samaria?" (John 4:9). In His response, Jesus knew the woman longed for love, respect, and restoration. He spoke of the hope He could offer. "If you knew who I was, you would have asked me to give you living water so that your thirst will be satisfied. It will become a spring of water within you, welling up to eternal life" (paraphrased).

The words stirred the woman deeply; she was so thirsty! "Sir, give me this water!"

Only now did Jesus open a door that brought her face-to-face with her sin and longing. He asked her to bring her husband to the well. The woman, likely desiring to maintain a relationship to this man, answered with a partial truth, that she had no husband. Only then did Jesus reveal that He knew far more about her life than she could have imagined. She realized that Jesus had known all this from the beginning—a prophet who did not condemn her for being a Samaritan woman nor for her life of sin. It was a transformative encounter; she immediately went to call others to come and meet Him.

As we discipline our children, we can learn from Christ's example. He did not approach the Samaritan woman with harshness. He responded gently, demonstrating His unhurried respect and love.

Our children have the same longings the woman had—to be seen, loved, heard, valued, and restored. Jesus revealed to the woman the goodness that is rooted in our deepest desires and longings. He is the living water. Just as Jesus provided exactly what the Samaritan woman needed, He will give us what we need. We cannot do this through our own strength. Jesus needs to fill us up before we can, in turn, pour into our own children.

STOPLIGHT REFLECTIONS

1. Can you think of a situation when your child regularly flips into Red or Yellow? Looking beyond the behavior, what could be behind your child regularly going into Yellow or Red Brain?

2. Observe and analyze your children. Think about how your rules and expectations might be adjusted for each child,

depending on their age and personality. How would this thinking influence specific parenting decisions?

3. Begin to read through the Gospels to see what kind of a listener Jesus is. Who does He take time to listen to? How deeply did He listen? How did He use questions to listen more deeply? Ask Jesus to nudge you when you need to pause and attend more deeply to your children. He will do it!

4. A mentor recently reminded me, "More people come to the Lord through 'honey' as opposed to 'the stick.'" Gentle words have a more healing effect than harsh ones. Use this imagery to help you evaluate how you might be too rigid in your rules or too harsh in your tone of voice. This week, try encouraging your child through the use of nurturing words and listening ears.

Prayer

Dear God, how I long to perceive my children as You do! I pray for Your grace to see them through Your eyes. You are truly beautiful; You are full of grace and truth! Help me to receive from You, grace upon grace.

CHAPTER 10

Coaching: Parenting for Green

"Mom! Thomas is sticking his toe in my ear!"

Comments of disgust, laughter, and annoyance quickly filled the van.

"Thomas, sticking toes in other people's ears is very gross. Please don't do that." *Well, that's a first.*

I stopped myself before scolding him further because I suspected he probably wasn't deliberately trying to do something wrong. He likely saw the toe poke as a sort of loving teasing of his sister. The root of the behavior was in Green, even though it was putting my daughter (and me) into Yellow. We had been in the van all day, driving home after a family trip, and everyone was overtired and bored. Thomas was especially bored.

"Mom, he's still bugging me!"

So I began distracting everyone with a snack. Thomas's

behavior was ratcheting up to defiance. Maybe once Thomas had something to do, he would stop bugging his sister.

It worked. For a few minutes.

"Mom! Thomas is . . ."

I turned around in my seat to address my son. "Okay, Thomas, you have two choices. You can either stop bothering your sister or come sit in the front row with me. Which one do you choose?"

The toe pokes stopped, along with the teasing and screeching and disgusted comments. The overall volume level of the van settled to normal. I was glad that Thomas decided to cooperate. If he hadn't, I was expecting to have him sit next to me up front so I could reconnect with him. I might then be able to send him back to his seat to play a game with his younger siblings. If it had gotten to that point where he deliberately disobeyed me, there would be a clear consequence that followed the reconnection.

I never know what kind of situations I will be faced with as a mother, but I work hard to know my disciplining tools so that I'm fully equipped!

What Do I Do When They Misbehave?

Stoplight parenting does not promote permissiveness, but how does a parent shift focus from punishing kids' misbehavior to training them to make better decisions?

Often, when we see inappropriate behavior, our natural reaction is to become angry and infuse fear and shame into our children. Remember, this will ultimately be counterproductive as it will send the child into Red or Yellow, and their capacity to learn will be compromised. As Stoplight parents, we want to keep ourselves and our children in Green to allow for learning as we correct the Yellow or Red root of the behavior.

So, as mentioned before, first try to determine if your child is acting out of a Red, Yellow, or Green Brain state. Once we have determined the root of the behavior, we can respond appropriately. Remember, Green-rooted misbehavior needs coaching, Yellow roots need connection, and Red roots need calming. Let's look at some specific strategies for coaching your child when the root of misbehavior is Green.

What Is a Coach?

I saw Rachel with a kitten. She loved the kitten but had apparently never been taught that holding it by its throat might not be the best idea. I bent down next to Rachel. "What a nice kitty!" I said as I gently yet quickly put the kitten in my lap, saving it from an unpleasant and uncomfortable (for the kitten) hug. "See, Rachel," I said as I began stroking the kitten. "Gentle hands for the kitty. Gentle hands. Do you want to try?" Rachel began petting the kitten, looking very pleased with herself.

Hours later, Rachel came up to me. With a big smile, she started petting my hands. "Gentle hands!" she exclaimed.

A successful bit of coaching, if I do say so myself!

In sports, a good coach builds a relationship with each player, seeking to grow player skills by building on their strengths while also addressing their weakness. A good coach has a strategy for working together as a team and a game plan for the future. A good coach is present, engaged, and encouraging, and he requires discipline and hard work from his players.

As coaches, parents have similar characteristics, making their relationship with their child their first priority even as they guide them toward better decisions. Parents who coach will practice and plan ahead for situations that are difficult —like bedtime. They are actively engaged—not just yelling "Knock it off" from the other room. Stoplight parents think about why behavior happens so we can address the actual problem, not just change behavior in the moment. We set a plan in place for long-term outcomes.

It is important to note that the vast majority of child misbe-havior does come from a Green Brain state. That may sound off, but we must remember that even when a child is in a healthy, Green state with fully operational intellectual capacity, they can still choose poorly. Disobedience doesn't go away just because a child is in Green. They may not even be considering boundaries and consequences. So when their basketball bounces away into the street, the immediate "I need my ball back" objective causes them to forget to even think that going into the street is dangerous and disobedient. It's forgotten in the fun of the moment.

If we overreact to a Green-rooted misbehavior, we send the child into Yellow or even Red, and may lose the opportunity to teach them in that moment. A child's neocortex is still very much under development, and this is why they need you, their coach, to help them learn.

Try, Try Again

"Yes, we're home!"

"I'm getting out first!"

"No! It's my turn to open the door!"

"Stop pushing me!"

I sighed as I turned off the car. When will they learn to leave the car without having a boxing match on the way out? I got out of the car and opened the house door myself before the kids could escalate to Yellow.

"Okay, time for a redo!" I called out.

The kids sighed, fully aware of what they had done and what I needed them to do. They climbed back into their seats in the car. I smiled as one by one they exited the vehicle without yelling, each child waiting for the brother or sister in front of them to go first. It worked this time, because the kids were all mostly in Green and were able to handle a redo then and there. Another time, most of the kids were in Yellow and maybe trending Red, so we had to reconnect and have a little something to eat first. After snack time, when everybody was in Green, we all went back out to the car for our redo.

Creating New Pathways in the Brain

The redo strategy is a wonderful way to practice expected and desired behavior. It gives children another shot at remembering what their attitude and behavior should be, to try responding to the same situation in the correct way.

A redo can happen only if the child and the parent are in Green Brain. At first, redos may take a while for children to understand, so you may have to instruct them in exactly what you want them to do. The more you use this strategy in your home, the more your children will understand right away what you want them to do when you ask, "Can you please do a redo?"

Like a family creating a pathway through long grass, trying something new starts off difficult, each step requiring a lot of effort.

After a few days of repeatedly walking on that same path, the grass begins to bend, and your direction become clear. Soon, the grass is completely packed down; the pathway is enjoyable to walk on.

In brain science, this is called creating neuropathways. Redos create these neuropathways in the brain. The first redo for a particular situation is day one of walking through the tall grass. The more the redo strategy is used for that situation, the stronger the neuropathway becomes, and the easier it is to remember the right choice.

Redirecting through Play

If a child is happily in Green Brain but their behavior is not appropriate, a playful redirection may be all that is needed. Do the unexpected: change your voice to something humorous, change your accent, say a silly phrase, pretend to be a well-known cartoon character, or sing your instructions. Make bedtime a game instead of a dreaded chore, asking who is going to be the quietest bunny tonight? If your kids are anything like mine, they can be full of energy, running around the house nonstop. Instead of yelling at them to stop, I say, "Looks like you have a lot of energy! Time to run five laps around the yard!"

With older kids especially, humor is an important tool for correcting behavior while keeping the mood fun and lighthearted. Teenagers have a keen sense of justice, so if we directly confront misbehavior that was done innocently, they will very quickly become confrontational. Instead, ask questions. Let them come up with solutions and answers that are their own. Remember, the goal here is to maintain the relationship, keeping the context of learning collaborative and fun.

Let's Play!

Play is an important tool to remember as you plan for potentially difficult coaching situations. Think ahead to what causes stress in your home, what has the potential to throw your children (and you) into Yellow or Red.

Here's one: When it's time to clean up the house! That used to be a bit of a nightmare for our family, but a little organization helped a lot. My husband creates zones in our house, and after every person or group cleans their zone, we all share a treat.

Homework can be another stress. Instead of it being a chore, motivate your kids with a game of hide-and-seek with Mom and Dad after they are finished!

Sometimes getting your kids to brush their teeth feels more like pulling teeth. Say this rhyme while brushing to make it fun: "Up like the garden, down like the rain, back and forth like a choo-choo train!" Have fun coming up with little ways you can decrease stress by increasing play in your home!

Natural Consequences

As often as possible, when misbehavior occurs, let the consequences be a natural result of the behavior. If your child is being silly at the dinner table and spills his food, it is natural that he will have to clean it up. If a child drops something on the ground, naturally, she will need to pick it up and put it where it belongs. You don't need to speak in anger because you are simply stating a fact. The same goes for when your child comes home from school with a pen that he does not own; it is clear that your child shouldn't keep that pen. Instead, she must return it to the owner and apologize. Natural consequences do not have to be complicated or exaggerated.

Stern scolding and yelling are unnecessary. These things usually only result in pushing both the child and parent into Yellow or Red Brain. Speak gently with love, ensuring that the natural consequences become a learning experience. Your child can learn appropriate behaviors without you yelling or being stern! I promise! In fact, raising your voice can push your child toward Yellow or Red Brain, significantly reducing their learning capabilities. Using a gentle, calm, lighthearted tone of voice is a much more effective way of getting your child to exhibit the behavior you want to see.

Mom's White Quilt

Green-rooted behavior can sometimes lead to Yellow and Red situations. When I ask my son Peter to take out the garbage, I don't always check up on him because my expectation is that he will do it. But he might forget, and his forgetfulness begins to influence everyone else. When I notice the garbage piling up, it puts me into Yellow Brain. I trusted him to do his chore, and now I see more work and mess. In these frustrating situations, I really need God's wisdom to help me not to condemn my child. My natural tendency is to shame him in these situations. Yes, there may be consequences for these "I forgot" scenarios, but getting mad at him won't help him remember any better. Instead, I can come up with strategies to help him remember. I can come alongside him and teach him.

Let me give you another example. While we were living in Uganda, my daughters Beth and Jessica called me outside and said, "Mommy, we're putting on a play!" I stared in horror at the sheets, towels, and special white quilt from my bedroom, all spread out on the red Ugandan dirt. Our foster kids and the neighborhood kids were there too, enjoying themselves and playing on the "stage." Did I mention that there were also eight puppies sitting on my white quilt?

I was horrified. I looked at all the dirty white laundry and saw so much work. *How dare my kids go into my room and take my sheets and my quilt,* I thought. I felt betrayed and violated.

But then I saw that my children were working together and collaborating. They are being inclusive. They probably were in

Green Brain, but I really couldn't see that! I only felt a sense of betrayal, as if my kids had intentionally done this to hurt me.

Children don't have the capacity to understand all the consequences in every situation. They likely didn't realize that using mom's white quilt as a stage to cover red dirt might result in a whole lot of cleaning!

I had two options—I could condemn them and tell them that what they'd done is awful, or I could see the good of what they had done and use it as an opportunity to teach, perhaps by making them a part of the whole cleaning process or some other way of showing that there are natural consequences to our actions. I could also help them understand my perspective. One of my biggest Red "buttons" is pushed when I see more work being created. When this happens, I need God's healing touch, guidance, and direction. I can trust that He is walking alongside me to help me stay in Green in these Yellow and Red situations!

Scripts and Mantras

Sometimes natural consequences are not applicable. The children aren't sharing, they are touching things in a store, they are jumping on the couch. One thing that helps to keep families and children focused and on the same page is having a short phrase—a script or a mantra—that represents the basic morals, values, and expectations of the members of the family. If your children know what kind of family you are and that this is something you have already agreed upon together, they will more readily seek to work toward that goal.

State a script or mantra that contradicts the inappropriate behavior, and they will know exactly what they are supposed to do and how they are to act.

"What kind of family are we?" is a simple little question I've used when kids are using rude words. It helps my kids realize that they were not showing respect and that they should adjust their words to be more respectful. "Use your words" is another phrase I'll use when the kids are acting out or physically fighting instead of talking about issues considerately.

When kids are jumping on the furniture: "Where do our feet go?"

"On the floor."

When they're touching items in a store: "Where do our hands go?"

"In our pockets."

By repeating simple family scripts, children eventually begin to recognize the correct behavior parents desire. Even better, they begin to practice that behavior.

Drawing Close to Your Child

Sometimes, words are unnecessary. Our children may simply need our presence to get on the right track and stay focused. When we're not present and engaged, kids are more likely to misbehave. When we hear or see that they are acting out, we can simply move closer to them without saying much of anything. So give them "a look" to communicate that they are misbehaving, and that they need to stop.

One advantage of being close is that you can also catch them doing the right thing. If you see behavior that you want repeated, thank them for it. Give a little praise. And make sure to name the specific behavior, "Thank you for sharing your chips with your brother," not, "Thank you for being a good boy."

Whether you are asking your children to stop an inappropriate action or you are expressing appreciation to them for carrying out an appropriate behavior, the attention and the positive reinforcement encourages them to repeat the behavior in the future. Instead of focusing on negative behavior, praise your children when they engage in the correct behavior you want to see.

I like to use a little ratio when I work with kids, which you may find helpful as a guide to observing good behavior. For every negative correction you give a child, point out nine positive behaviors of that same child.

Body Regulation

Physical activity is a great way to let out built-up energy. It releases hormones called endorphins, which can positively affect mood and behavior. Positive physical activity is always an appropriate deterrent when the child has shown inappropriate behavior. For instance, running laps outside around the house or doing jumping jacks are excellent ways to deter your child from acting in an inappropriate manner. The point is to provide a safe outlet for the energy or anger, not to make him angrier. So be careful not to become a drill sergeant!

Even if unintentional, reconciliation is always needed if somebody has been hurt while someone was in Green root.

Coaching using playful engagement is an excellent way of keeping children in Green Brain. By using this approach, you will minimize the number of times you have to go any further with discipline. However, sometimes children will not respond to this. And if their initial behavior was rooted in Yellow, a less playful, more firm response is required.

Going Deeper

Finally, brothers, whatever is true, whatever is honorable,
whatever is just, whatever is pure, whatever is lovely,
whatever is commendable, if there is any excellence, if there
is anything worthy of praise, think about these things.
PHILIPPIANS 4:8

Imagine a typically busy day in your household. You come into the living room to find it has been completely rearranged into a giant fort constructed from furniture, pillows, sheets, and blankets. You can't believe it. You're having guests for dinner this evening, and reconstructing the living room certainly wasn't in your preparation plans!

Unfortunately, you flip immediately from Green Brain into Red Brain. And the angry words tumble out: "What were you thinking? You just made a huge mess! I can't believe you've done this!"

Sometime later, when you've had more distance from the moment, you realize that your children didn't act from bad motives, but were simply being children. Sure, they were disruptive, but in such a creative, imaginative, and thoroughly childlike way. It had been so easy to focus on the disruption and lose sight of the pure, lovely, and admirable characteristics right in front of you.

It would have been such a delight to witness firsthand Jesus interacting with kids. Imagine what kind of dad He might have been, had that been part of God's plan to save mankind. We do catch a glimpse of Him with children in the Gospels, in which we see His view of childhood as well as the need to learn from children how to live as His disciples.

In Luke 18:15-17, we read that a great crowd of people was pressing in on Jesus. Along with the sick jostling for His attention, there were Pharisees and other important men wanting to speak with Him. In the midst of the confusion were several parents, holding out their children to Him. The disciples indignantly ordered them to move aside, but Jesus eagerly called after the parents, "Let the little children come to me, . . . for the kingdom of God belongs to such as these" (NIV).

Jesus took the children, put His hand on their heads and blessed them! Rather than seeing them as interruptions, He longed to be with them, longed to bless them. They refreshed His spirit!

I fully expect that He knelt to their eye level so they might see, laugh, and talk with Him. I imagine the tone of playfulness in His voice. Children know and delight in those who delight in them!

Then He said something else interesting: "Truly I tell you, anyone who will not receive the kingdom of God like a little child will never enter it" (Luke 18:17, NIV). I find this so interesting. What is it about being childlike that Jesus is calling us to embrace if we are to live under the reign of God? In what ways is Jesus calling us to actually learn from our children?

Children are vulnerable, of course. I think this means we must take care to let down our defenses and risk being vulnerable with others and with God. Children are wondrously open to others, to new experiences, to joy, wonder, and imagination. That same boundless trust and receptivity is key in our ability to receive the life of the Father, Son, and Holy Spirit.

Furthermore, children know that they are needy; they cannot make their way on their own. May we, too, abandon our illusions that we can be the parents that we long to be without the strength of the Holy Spirit and the community of God.

Finally, children are generous, withholding judgment and giving their love and forgiveness freely. May God, in His grace, free us to live so generously and compassionately! May we have the grace to see God through our children's eyes, to see what is true, noble, right, pure, lovely, and admirable. May we not only celebrate it, but with God's help, allow it to shape our own lives. Good parents are themselves childlike!

STOPLIGHT REFLECTIONS

1. Do you ever use a playful voice to redirect your child? How effective do you find a little humor and playfulness in calling your child back to responsible, wise behavior?

2. How have natural consequences worked in your home? What is challenging about linking misbehavior to a clear, understandable consequence?

3. Spend a few minutes visualizing Jesus on the hillside. As He sees you, His face lights up. There are others who would edge you away from Him, but He reaches out for you. You can see in His eyes that He knows all about you, the good as well as the rough edges. He does not flinch, but you see that His love encompasses all of who you are. Forgiveness flows from Him. You are His child!

Prayer

Father, You have given us the power to be called Your children!
Like my own children, I too can be disruptive, messy and
challenging! Help me slow down so I can receive Your blessing
upon me. Help me see Your delight in me, Your child.
Thank You for the joy of parenthood! Thank You for the humor,
fresh perspectives on reality, and quirky expressions of who You are!
Thank You for ensuring that I do not take myself too seriously!
Help me to remain flexible, curious and open to continuing
new glimpses of who You are through my children!

CHAPTER 11

Connection: Parenting for Yellow

IT HAD BEEN A FUN EVENING. Our kids and their friends played happily while we parents reconnected—talking and laughing until it was *way* past bedtime. And now we were paying the price. It started on the drive home with the whining and fussing. We knew it would only escalate when we walked through the front door.

A block from home, my husband pulled the car over, and I turned to face the kids, "Okay, guys, we had a fun evening, and now we are all tired and hungry. Do you think we can work together? I'll go get a small, special snack ready while you all put on your PJs. After snack, if you can get your teeth brushed and get into bed in five minutes, then you can have a few minutes of book time before lights out. Sound like a good plan? Everyone ready to work together?"

We pulled into the driveway. Everyone scampered into the house and up the stairs. They were back before I finished setting out the apples and peanut butter. Fifteen minutes later, I gave each child a goodnight hug as I turned out the lights. Not too shabby!

Granted, not every late night has happened this way. Too often, I forget or am unable to get to Green myself, and in the chaos of trying to get a bunch of tired, hungry kids to bed quickly, I end up turning out the lights on frustrated and disconnected kids.

If we are looking to parent in relationship, we need to really understand the roots (the hidden motivators) underneath the outward behavior. While sometimes this seems obvious (like when they are tired), often we need to look deeper to discover what is really going on. Once again, Stoplight starts with you—you need to get yourself to Green first to be ready to use your full thinking power to understand and address the situation.

Misbehavior that is rooted in Yellow is the result of some combination of three things: unmet needs, unsolved problems, or a lack of skills. So how do we respond to this reality? Many parents might immediately jump to dishing out consequences—taking away privileges, scolding, raising their voices. A better way is to take a breath, connect with them, then address the need, problem, or skill that is lacking. In the story above, they are hungry and tired—two unmet needs. If I respond to the first need with a snack and meet their need for connection with a call for teamwork, I can more quickly meet their need for sleep. Not only will they get to bed sooner, but if they have been helped back to Green Brain, rather than escalating to Red, they are in a better state for actually falling asleep!

Unmet needs are often the easiest Yellow root to address, especially if the need is physical. We all know it is a bad idea to take a hungry toddler to the grocery store—we are just asking for a temper tantrum in the cookie aisle. Toddlers and preschoolers need to eat every two to three hours, and growing teens perhaps just as often. In our home, we keep a bowl filled with fruit and healthy snacks on the counter. The kids are allowed to grab something from the bowl so long as they ask first. This was particularly important for one of our kids. When he first came to live with us, he often seemed to panic, saying, "I'm hungry, I'm hungry." I would point him to the bowl of bananas, and he would calm down.

Fatigue is another need that often causes Yellow-rooted behavior. Are your kids getting ten hours of sleep a night? If the bedtime routine is a nightly battle, consider moving bedtime up by half an hour and see if getting ready for bed a little earlier, when they are a little less tired, helps. This makes the mornings go easier too.

Consider whether the unmet need that is causing Yellow-rooted behavior is an emotional need. Studies show that stress and anxiety in children, especially teenagers, are at an all-time high. Maybe they just need a hug. Perhaps the environment is too stimulating; turn off the TV, turn off (or on) the music, turn down the lights, decrease the clutter. If your child is older, have a conversation—when they are in Green Brain—and ask them what they think might help.

Once you have identified and addressed the need and the child is back to Green, you need to decide whether the situation requires further intervention. If the tired child yelled at their brother, they still need to go back and mend their mistake. If a hungry child wouldn't help with dinner cleanup, then maybe they need to help you wash the dishes after dinner. Remember, the goal is not revenge for the past but training for the future. So the conversation is not, "You didn't help clean up the toys, so now you have extra chores after dinner," but rather, "I know you were really hungry before dinner, and that made it hard for you to help with cleaning up. I did your share to help you out. Now it is time for you to help me with my after-dinner clean up. We are a family that helps each other."

Unsolved Problems

Discovering unsolved problems takes a little more investigation. We naturally do this with infants, working through their need for food, warmth, or a new diaper. Once we are sure we have met all their needs, if they are still crying, we look further and start to wonder about teething or gas pain. Some problems require parental intervention—like grieving the loss of a pet or not understanding the math homework. Other times, just by listening, the burden is lifted; or asking the right question can guide our children to discovering the solution for themselves—like friendship squabbles or being upset that Daddy just left on a trip. Loss and grief can often be expressed as frustration or anger. Help your child identify that the frustration they are feeling about their sibling's irritating behavior might have more to do with Grandpa and Grandma leaving that morning.

Remember, the overarching need of the Yellow Brain is to feel connected, valued, seen, and heard. As you work through the unsolved problem, you want to:

- Understand—Ask questions, think about triggers, think big (bullying) and small (left homework at school)
- Validate—Acknowledge emotions (that they are in Yellow), model empathy
- Brainstorm—Since we need to be in Green to really problem-solve, this might just be a short-term solution

Lacking Skills

Children lack various skills at various stages of life. They come into the world not knowing how to walk, talk, or care for themselves, and one of our jobs as parents is to give them the skills they need to be healthy, functional adults. Since we learn best in Green Brain, that is the time and space for a child to successfully do any skill building.

However, sometimes the lack of a specific skill will result in Yellow-rooted behavior. How do we help a child in Yellow who lacks the necessary skills to handle a situation? And how do we do so without escalating that situation?

It isn't easy, but it starts—as all responses to Yellow do—with connection—eye contact, a gentle touch on the arm, perhaps a hug. It's best to avoid the popular time-out for a child in Yellow. Instead, practice time-in. Perhaps your daughter isn't sharing toys with siblings or friends. Sitting her on the stairs to "think about" her behavior does nothing to teach her the skill of sharing or empathy, and it isolates her from the person that she is supposed to be learning these skills from—you. Rather, have her help you prepare a snack for the other kids. You have still removed her from the group, which communicates to her that her behavior is not appropriate— and it keeps the other kids from going into Yellow—but you have maintained and perhaps even strengthened your relationship with her. And by engaging in an activity of service, you have planted seeds of empathy and caring—skills she needs to work on.

Time-in is important for all ages, but it looks different for each developmental stage. Time-in with a toddler might mean they sit in their high-chair in the kitchen while you make dinner and talk with them. The school-age child, who was fighting with siblings, joins you to help make dinner. The teenager who has been disrespectful goes with Dad to the grocery store to pick up milk. The common factor is the physical and emotional closeness of the parent and child. Whereas time-out isolates and distances the child and parent, time-in strengthens that relationship. Notice, too, that while the point is to spend time with your child—building skills, modeling empathy and love, while keeping everyone safe—that doesn't necessarily mean life has to stop.

Choices, Choices

A valuable tool for parenting a Yellow-rooted child is choices. Remember, a child in Yellow is easily overwhelmed and is not thinking clearly. Focus the attention on two good choices, "Do you want to do your homework at the kitchen table or at the desk?" Stoplight parents will see that a question like "Do you want to do your homework or go to bed without dinner?" is not a valid choice.

What types of choices should you offer your child? First, both options need to be something you're fine with. Both need to accomplish the task at hand. And both options need to be something the child might want to do.

A child doesn't need to be in Yellow to offer choices, of course, but this is a helpful tool for this brain state. Not only does it bring simplicity to the situation, but it also gives the child a measure of control and the feeling of value and worth, which is what the Yellow Brain desperately needs.

Compromises

Sometimes a child may come back with another alternative. In our home, we allow and encourage these sorts of compromises. We've found that they teach children to have a voice and to think outside the box. But they have to first ask, "May I have a compromise?" So maybe in the above situation, they ask for a compromise: "Can I do my homework on the porch?"

You do not need to agree to the compromise. Maybe the porch is a fun but seriously distracting environment, away from your supervision, and you know very little schoolwork will get done out there. On the other hand, maybe being outside is a great place for this particular child to get their work done. If the compromise they ask for accomplishes the task at hand, say, "Yes!" and praise the good thinking. However, asking for compromises can often become a stalling technique for some kids, so we usually only allow one chance to propose a compromise. Don't let continual negotiations drag down wise time use.

Once the child is back in Green Brain and ready to learn, find a way to practice whatever skill was lacking in the moment. If they threw a tantrum because they couldn't do operate a zipper, practice operating zippers. If they got overwhelmed and anxious, have a glass of water and a snack, and then practice deep breathing.

Addressing Yellow-rooted behavior takes a lot of insight and creative thinking. Remember, in the Spotlight Approach, Yellow means, "Slow Down, Caution, Watch Out." Be very present and aware so that the child doesn't escalate to Red Brain. Some children have very small windows of Yellow, so catching them before they get to Red is incredibly difficult. But, as you and they learn to read their body's signs, you will increase their awareness, and they can ask for help getting back to Green before flipping to Red.

Branches Connected to the Vine

Abide in me as I abide in you.

JOHN 15:4, NRSV

As a parent, I am often tired. There are so many motherly demands, so many needs and wants, and my stress level increases as I think of all these people who depend on me. And on top of all that, I often stay up too late, using that little sliver of peace and quiet in my day to clean, work, and sort out my life with fewer interruptions. It's easy to find myself in Yellow when I let the stress of parenting get the best of me! I need to stop trying to do things in my own strength and take time to reconnect with God and focus on the rest I can find in Him.

Yellow Brain is all about the need for connection, and the desire for connection often deteriorates into desire for power and control: "I'm going to make you sit nicely with me at the breakfast table! I'm going to make you talk to me respectfully!"

When we experience disconnection and go into Yellow, we try to gain some level of control in any way we can. But this control is not possible until things are right within us. I can't make others connect with me, but I can stop and recenter myself in God's presence. By doing this, I reconnect with God, remembering that my identity and self-worth are in Him and not in my unsolved problems.

Too often I want things to happen in my time and at my own pace. If I can stop in the middle of these situations and pray that God will change my perspective, He can help me to understand and see my life through His eyes.

Yellow Brain means we are stressed, tired, disconnected. We need Jesus. "I am the vine; you are the branches. Whoever abides in me and I in him, he it is that bears much fruit, for apart from me you can do nothing" (John 15:5).

I love how the famous South African pastor and writer Andrew Murray elaborates on this:

> Come, let us set ourselves at His feet and meditate on His word, with an eye fixed on Him alone. Let us set ourselves quietly before Him, waiting to hear His holy voice—the still small voice that is mightier than the storm—as He speaks, "Abide in Me." The soul that truly hears Jesus speak receives power to accept and to hold the blessing He offers.[1]

We cannot love our children well when we are disconnected from Jesus. A parent in Yellow Brain needs connection with Jesus just as much as a child in Yellow Brain needs connection with a parent or caregiver. Recognizing the stress, anxiety, exhaustion, and depletion of Yellow Brain is an invitation to come back to Jesus and receive the love, comfort, and care that is found in Him. Drawing near to Jesus doesn't magically make all our challenges go away, but it does remind us that we are heard, seen, valued, and loved in the midst of those challenges.

STOPLIGHT REFLECTIONS

1. Think of a situation that sends your kids (or you) to flip into Yellow. What are the unmet needs, unsolved problems, and lacking skills that need to be addressed? Think of options you might offer your child in that situation. (Remember, the options must both be good from the child's perspective but also need to accomplish the task/

goal.) Also, brainstorm how you can do more "time-ins" with your children in age-appropriate ways.

2. Read the following verses and reflect on what God might be saying to us concerning being in a Yellow state:
    Matthew 6:26 (unmet needs)
    Psalms 46 (unsolved problems)
    James 1:5 (lacking skills).

―――――――――― *Prayer* ――――――――――

Shepherd God, You prepare a table before me in the midst of
my enemies of frustration, loneliness, impatience, exhaustion.
You give me Your very self! Help me recognize when
my children need the same grace that You give to me.
In Your name,
Amen.

CHAPTER 12

Calming: Parenting for Red

My daughter slammed the door and stormed out of the room. The cat was standing on the table, enjoying all of the crumbs my children had left from lunch. Then . . . *smack!* The cat went flying! My child, in a rage about something else, had swatted the cat right off the table!

"Why don't you go swing on the hammock for a bit?" I said. "I think that will make you feel better."

I checked to make sure the cat wasn't injured and then sat down on the veranda, watching my daughter from a distance. After she had calmed down, I went over to talk to her. We talked about her reasons for being angry. She did feel bad about slamming the door and hitting the cat, but consequences were still needed. We first practiced a redo, gently petting the cat and closing the door normally, and then we had a little time of reconnection as she helped me make school lunches for the next day.

As a parent, you cannot address Red-rooted behavior while a child is *in* Red. So as hard as it might be, stop talking, stop trying to solve the problem, stop correcting behavior, stop trying to proceed with the task at hand, stop everything. A child in Red is reacting to a perceived threat. This threat may be physical or emotional, and it may be very real. Their brother was hitting them. They are super tired, and someone broke their toy. Or maybe they are thrown into a panic when they see a dog after having been previously bitten. So what do we do?

First, remember that Red Brain requires calming.

Safety First

If there is any immediate threat to their safety or the safety of others around them, address that first. Assess the situation and decide whether you need to remove the child in Red or remove others. If your preschooler is running toward the street, scoop them up. If your teenager is screaming at their sibling, have the sibling leave the room. The one in Red is unlikely to be able to follow directions, so asking them to leave may just cause further friction and not help get others safe. Once immediate threats to safety are addressed, there are three things you do need to walk through with a child in Red.

Parenting a child who is in Red Brain can trigger so many emotions within parents. When my child is in Red, my natural response is to go into Red Brain myself. I sometimes feel very fearful when this happens. Then we have two people using only half of their intelligence, and no progress can be made. When I go into Red, my child feels unsafe and judged. Both of us will say hurtful and unkind things. This escalates the issue and begins to create a rift in our relationship, since I cannot support them unconditionally in these Red Brain moments. I am also tempted to put more shame on my children when they go into Red Brain.

Sometimes I don't even realize that I am doing this. Maybe my daughter has messed up at the dinner table, and I say, "What were you thinking?"

Maybe you've said similar words to your child. To my daughter, that wording always comes across as something like, "What kind of idiot are you?"

Or maybe I enter the kitchen and see that my daughter hasn't washed the dishes that she said she had finished. I might say to her, "Look at the kitchen! Do you really think this is clean?" These responses unintentionally make my daughter feel shame, especially when I say these things in front of other family members. This communicates to my daughter that I don't think she is good enough. My daughter will likely respond defensively by going into Red and yelling at me. She is not feeling safe and secure, and she will not be able to admit her mistakes unless she is in Green.

How does God react when we mess up and go into Red? Does He see us as not quite good enough? Does He shame us by saying, "What were you thinking?" No—He comes alongside us and invites us to come to Him. If I have an image of God that He will never see me as good enough, I will also feel shame—and I will want to turn my face away and hide. Shame means I am focusing on myself. I am not holding up my actions against who I want to be and developing moral identity. But God is a compassionate and loving God. He is beautiful, good, and true. I need to have this view in order to show the same love and compassion to my children.

When in the Red

First step: Help the child to recognize and name their brain state. We begin the calming process by naming the emotion or brain state because this causes the brain to release calming neurotransmitters that begin to soothe the Red Brain. Dan Seigel talks more about the science of why this is important and sums it up as "Name It to Tame It," as we talked about previously.

The Process of Keeping Yourself in Green

Secondly, remind them to breathe. If you have talked about this when the child was previously in Green Brain you can remind them to take slow, deep breaths as they practiced. However, if you suddenly tell them to take a deep breath without prior practice and teaching, they may be more resistant, and it can escalate the situation further.

Thirdly, help them self-regulate. Repetitive physical movement helps us regulate, but self-regulation is a learned skill, so children may need help to do this either by suggestion or with our physical presence. A younger child may need to be held and rocked until they calm down. For the teen, this might be accomplished by going out to shoot some hoops or going for a brisk walk. If you have swings or a trampoline, having the child in Red go swing or jump is a great way to help them regulate internally. Self-regulation works best if you have worked out a plan with the child ahead of time about what they can do when they are in Red. This way, when you detect Red-rooted behavior, you can say, "It looks like you might be in Red. Remember, you were going to try getting back to Green by rocking in the rocking chair. I'm right here if you need a hug." Every child is different. Some children do better if they can be alone to process and calm down. (Note that this is different than a time-out as it is the child's choice to remove themselves from the situation—and their choice about when to reintegrate.) Other children want and need the physical closeness of the parent and may do best with physical touch in the form of a foot or back rub as they work their way back to Green.

It is incredibly important, during this time, for you to stay in Green. This can be difficult. We are wired to mirror the brain states of those around us, and even to respond in Red when we see another person is Red. This is natural because the Red Brain fires up when it feels unsafe or when our loved ones feel unsafe. Resist this tendency. If you can stay calmly in Green, your child's brain will eventually get the message that everything is alright and start to calm down too.

As they move from Red, through Yellow, to Green, you may notice them transitioning from "mad to sad." Anger gives way to tears. As Dr. Gordon Neufeld has explored in his book *Hold on to Your Kids: Why Parents Need to Matter More Than Peers,* this process is normal. He encourages us to see tears as a positive sign. The child's brain has begun processing information through the more emotional-focused limbic system rather than the more survival-oriented brain stem. Red Brain is giving away to Green, but it generally moves through Yellow first. You know you are on the right track if the screams turn to sobs, and yells become cries.[1]

Once a child is back in Green, you need to address the behavior—perhaps with a redo, an apology, or a natural consequence, all depending on the circumstance. However, do not act on this immediately, or the child is likely to escalate back to Red. At a minimum, a child needs fifteen minutes in a calm Green state before beginning to address the Red-rooted behavior. Often it will take longer. Of course, you likely need to investigate what the root cause or trigger was, and then brainstorm ideas for how to avoid it in the future.

Becoming a Stoplight parent is a process, one that takes a lot of practice and learning of new habits. Every day I am learning what it means to be a Stoplight parent. I am learning to discipline instead of punishing, and to see my children as safe and unsafe, rather than good or bad. I'm constantly learning about and rediscovering the principles in this book—and I'm the one writing it!

New challenges will arise, children change, disasters happen, and we'll all flip from Green to Red. It's by no means an easy job, but making parenting a priority is worth it. It's an investment. At the end of the day, we all want what is best for our children, and that alone can motivate us to continue practicing these tools and change our home into a Stoplight home. Don't quit! You can do this!

Remember the demon-possessed man in Mark chapter 5? There was a very Red guy in a very Red situation! He was completely out of control—so much so that he was hurting himself. The disciples feared him. The community feared him. But did Jesus fear him and go into Red? Of course not—He stayed very Green. Jesus recognizes evil for what it is. He is not afraid of our big Red emotions. And He wants to release us from the evil that is harming us. Sometimes our children get caught up with the wrong people. When we see evil at work in the lives of our kids, we become afraid. We go into Red. But we can't react out of fear. Jesus is big enough to handle the biggest Red moments any of us could ever have.

Holding Space

Peace I leave with you; my peace I give to you. Not as the world gives do I give to you. Let not your hearts be troubled, neither let them be afraid.

JOHN 14:27

I recently came across a YouTube video titled "Holding Space: Beautiful Two's." In the video, a two-year-old girl has a complete meltdown. She cries and cries, throwing herself on the floor. Meanwhile, the father is sitting on the floor next to her. He is present and gentle, waiting for his little girl to come to him. He loves her unconditionally, despite her meltdown.

The video reminds me that in the middle of our fits, God is there. Like the father in the video, God beckons us to come and rest with Him in the middle of our tantrums. When I'm angry at God, that's okay. I can share that with God. I can ask Him to help me in my unbelief! I might say, "I'm mad at You, God! I'm mad at the world! But please—just hold me." God is not going to judge me. He will just be there, waiting for me to surrender.

In the same way, I'm learning to restrain my tendency to judge my kids for their big emotions. When we are in Red, we want support. We want to be loved.

Sometimes my husband will come up to me and give me a hug when he senses me going into Red. The responsibilities of a parent can sometimes feel overwhelming.

When friends or other adults are having a meltdown, I don't yell at them to calm down or use force to stop them. I hug them. I tell them it's okay. So why can't I do this with my kids?

I don't expect my children to be perfect. I need to extend grace and try to repair the damage. Just like God extends grace to us in our Red-Brained moments! He sits beside us, holding space, inviting us to come to Him. He is always available: "Trust in him at all times, O people; pour out your heart before him; God is a refuge for us" (Psalm 62:8).

STOPLIGHT REFLECTIONS

1. Encourage your family to consider what a Green plan would look like for each personality, the path they might take to get back to Green when they've flipped to Red. Remember, enjoyable physical activities like jumping, rocking, bouncing, or walking are often the most effective.

2. Find a quiet place to sit with God. I like to light a candle to remind myself that Jesus is the light of my life and that He is present with me. Now, invite Him to shine His light in the dark places of your heart, illuminating the challenges that trouble you. "The true light, which gives light to everyone, was coming into the world. He was in the world, and the world was made through him, yet the world did not know him. He came to his own, and his own people did not receive him. But to all who did receive him, who believed in his name, he gave the right to become children of God" (John 1:9-12).

Prayer

Come, Spirit of God, and hold me when I am afraid. Your presence is peace. Come hold me when I am angry. Your presence is peace. Help me to breathe out my fear and anger into Your outspread arms. Help me to breathe in Your comfort, forgiveness, and love. From Your fullness may I hold my children. From Your fullness may they know Your peace.

CHAPTER 13

Protecting Our Children: Safety

It was a day to be remembered. It was the beginning of summer, and we had family visiting from out of town. To celebrate, we'd all gone to a large public pool to spend the day. We were swimming, splashing each other, playing ever so nicely. It was one of those moments I wish I could capture and relive again and again.

Two-year-old Peter had been playing by the side of the pool. I was talking to my mother, who was holding my youngest, but when I went back to the kids, there was no Peter. I asked my father, who was playing with one of the other children, about Peter's whereabouts, and he replied, "I thought he was with you."

My heart stopped. This was supposed to be a celebration, a day to remember as a happy time spent with the family—and I had just lost my youngest son! *He doesn't know how to swim! Has he drowned? Has he been kidnapped?*

Where was Peter? The family immediately began searching,

alerting every lifeguard on duty about the situation. By now, everyone in the pool grounds was aware of what was going on. I was frantic. I'm such a horrible mother! How could I have let this happen?

Radios were buzzing on and off. "No sign here. I'll check the bathrooms."

"Not here, either."

My mind kept flashing to images of Peter drowning in the pool, dying, gasping for breath. The lifeguards evacuated the pool and continued to search, but there was no body to be found. No body . . . That's a good sign, right? Means he's alive somewhere?

Or perhaps he's been kidnapped! Or he was hit by a car on the road! I could barely breathe. Twenty minutes passed—the longest twenty minutes of my life. Radios kept on buzzing, reporting no sightings until I was informed that there was a man carrying a small boy that matched the description of my son. My husband had decided to look outside the pool grounds, trying to see life from a two-year-old boy's perspective. Of course, Peter would run off to the park nearby! He loves the park!

I ran toward my husband and took Peter into my own arms and hugged him so tightly. I vowed never to let him out of my sight again! An impossible promise to keep, of course, but it remains in my heart to this day. I don't want anything terrible to happen to my children!

It's every parent's worst nightmare: losing your child. And not just losing your child, but losing your child and it being your fault! I'll always remember the people around me on that early summer afternoon. I wondered if they thought I was a horrible parent for not keeping a closer eye on my son. Of course, it was a simple lack of communication between my father and myself—a simple accident that could happen to anyone.

One of our most important jobs as parents is keeping our

children safe—not just physically but emotionally as well. That summer day, I was reminded again that young kids really do need full-time supervision. Maximizing supervision minimizes issues. And it's more than just keeping an eye on your babies. It's about minimizing the potential for your children to experience possibly traumatic circumstances. As our children grow up into their teenage years, their tendency is to distance themselves from us. This is a natural process to help them—and us—prepare to leave home when they are mature enough. Supervision is still important, of course, but it generally shifts toward coaching and helping our teens be mindful of the dangers they will face in the wider world. We're not directly protecting them so much as preparing them to have the strength and skills to thrive amid those dangers.

However, we must be vigilant to make sure that they do not spend excessive periods of time alone as they grow up. If we allow this, it increases the temptation for them to become involved in negative behaviors, since they are spending so much time away from the main positive influences in their lives. Significant periods of alone time increase the chances of our children viewing excessive or harmful media, participating in dangerous activities, or hanging out with negative influences. And by spending time with our children, we create close connections whereby our children feel safe to process the challenges of life with us.

Safe and loving Green Brain parents equip their kids to take a stand against the negative influences of the world, including peers and friends that tempt them into unsafe activities such as taking drugs and alcohol, viewing pornography, joining gangs, breaking the law, etc. Though there are many negative influences, there are two main areas that need our specific attention and are common no matter where we live in the world: media and peer influence.

Media

Any of form of media can be used to influence people for good or for ill, teaching positive or negative lessons, influencing them to behave in appropriate or inappropriate manners. It may, or may not, be surprising how much the media affects the worldview, beliefs, and areas of interest in the human mind. This is especially true when young minds are still forming and are more vulnerable to influence.

Yet translating this information into an action plan to protect our children can be difficult. These days, media is everywhere. Accessing the internet, movies, music, and television—along with all manner of advertisement—has never been easier. As parents, we need to be wary of how our kids use media—more than our own parents ever needed to be.

Media such as pornography has devastating effects on the human brain. It triggers the pleasure system of the brain, causing addiction, sometimes after the first exposure to it. Violent, vulgar, and explicit television shows, movies, books, and images can also have profoundly negative effects on our children, though these effects may not take hold as quickly. Over time, exposure to these negative influences eventually rewires the brain to accept violent and sexually explicit acts as acceptable, vulgar language and profanity as normal.

True, it's impossible to watch everything that our children do every hour of the day. And it would be too easy to say, "Just know what your children are doing on the internet and watching on television." There are, however, some safeguards we can put in place to form an action plan for minimizing the exposure our children have to the negative influences of media.

When the kids are young, you'll likely be able to get away with some basic principles such as not allowing kids to watch television or have access to the internet while you are away from them. Try to keep up with the movies, video games, and music your children have access to and have heard about from friends, so you're aware of what messages and images are going into your children's minds. Help your kids find positive media that aligns with your faith and family values. In our home, my husband and I monitor all of the movies our kids are watching. We also have a designated night that we sit down as a family to watch a movie everyone will enjoy.

Keep up with the latest accountability and filtering software applications for your computers and mobile devices. These programs—some free, some for a cost—help parents to monitor what young children are accessing online. When your children start getting their own devices, make sure you know how to keep up with the parental monitoring settings on each of the two main mobile operating systems.

Of course, the primary way to safeguard kids from harmful media is to consistently teach them what is healthy media and what is not. A big goal of our parenting is that the values we instill in our children will truly take root and be carried forward into adulthood. This happens through a connected, trusting relationship. Where there is a good attachment between you and your children, the morals you seek to pass on are more likely to stick.

The Importance of Positive Peers

The hope of every parent is to minimize the negative influences of peers and increase the positive influences that come from true friends. Just like with media, the best safeguarding technique is to teach our children how to wisely choose friends with whom they spend the majority of their time. Teaching them what kind of characteristics are positive and what kind of behaviors and attitudes are acceptable will help them be aware of what friends are safe to be around. It's true that we can't completely decide with whom our children spend every moment of their time—especially while they are at school—but we can certainly teach them to recognize the kind of friends that are going to help them make safe and wise decisions.

But leading them toward wisdom in their friendships is only part of the battle. Another way we increase positive peers and friends in our children's lives is by being interested and involved in their social life, getting to know the kids they see on their sports teams, the friends they hang out with after school. Allow them to come to your home. Get to know these kids. Get to know their parents. If one of my children makes a new friend at school, we try to be intentional by inviting not only the friend but their entire family over for supper. And we try to learn what kind of atmosphere the friends of our kids live in. Green, Yellow, or Red? What kind of activities do the children enjoy? These are the kinds of concerns we must be focused on if we are to minimize the negative influences from our children's peers and friends.

If our children are overeager to make new friends, they may be persuaded to engage in unsafe activities in order to "fit in" or feel accepted. Many parents notice this tendency when they move their family to a new town or city, or when children change schools and are more keenly interested in finding good friends.

Our children will be more vulnerable to peer pressure if we do not have a healthy attachment with them. When we don't spend enough time with our children, they will seek that attachment, love, and value from their peers, whether those friends are positive influences or not. In order to feel respected and valued, they may join the first group of friends that fills these needs.

In our home, we have an open house policy for our older kids' friends. They know they are allowed to drop by, eat supper with us, play with the younger kids, or even come along on family outings with us. In many ways, those friends have become part of our family. This open family policy has very much helped my husband and me nurture healthy influences in our kids' lives.

Teaching our Children to Protect Themselves

Helping kids feel emotionally safe in their relationships is a major goal of the Stoplight Approach. And while we cannot protect our kids in every situation, we can teach them how to identify whether a situation is safe or unsafe. And by giving them simple tools to respond to these various scenarios, we can help our children to protect themselves when we are not around to do so for them. Put simply, we must teach them to feel both safe on the inside and outside. This includes how to have a safe heart—by feeling safe, loved, and valued, as well as being able to trust. This also includes knowing how to have a safe body by welcoming adult protection during situations that have the potential to be physically harmful.

Stoplight gives children the language to communicate with parents. They may not know why a particular situation is bad, but they can identify that in that situation, they are starting to go into Yellow. As Stoplight parents, we teach our children to be tuned in to their emotional state and to recognize Yellow or Red Brain states. When we have created and developed a healthy attachment with our kids, they know they can come to us when the Stoplight signals are flipping.

Right and Wrong, Good and Evil

Our children's sense of right and wrong will be shaped by all of the above influences. Our job as parents is to ensure that our children learn what is right and wrong from positive influences. Keeping silent and having no discussions with our children about their physical safekeeping only harms them. Though talking about child protection with your children may not be easy for you, it is a simple way to empower them and lessen the power an abuser has over their lives.

It's important that our children know it's wrong for them to be beaten, or have their private parts touched (anywhere that their bathing suit goes), or to be forced into sexual activity. When they aren't taught that these activities are wrong, it is easier for them to be violated—especially if the abuse is performed by someone they trust. A perpetrator could groom a child into the behavior he wants and then convince them that it is their special secret. When the child matures and understands what really happened—or is still currently happening—he or she is bound by guilt and shame and will feel powerless to change the situation.

By cultivating a home culture of open discussion about what is right and wrong, we are giving our children the power to shout, "NO!" when someone tries to harm them. We are helping them to identify danger, giving them the power to identify that something inappropriate has happened, and granting them freedom to communicate it with people they trust.

Bullying

The bully, the target, and the bystander are the three types of people involved in bullying. Our kids need to recognize that they must tell a trusted adult if they are the target of bullying. This is a positive, proactive response to bullying—it doesn't encourage fighting or bullying back—and it should be encouraged in every school.

The bystander enables a bully to continue hurting others by not taking any action to help the target. If children know what bullying looks like, they must be empowered to stand up for those who are being bullied instead of watching or letting the bullying continue without intervention. Bystanders can act by telling a trusted adult, or even using kind, Green-focused words to talk the bully out of hurting the target. Bullies are more likely to stop if all of the bystanders defend the target. Teach your children the differences between each role, and they can help stop bullying in their school.

Of course, these basic guidelines will not work in every situation, but this framework can help parents build awareness, create discussion, and give children the tools they need to break the power of abuse and bullying.

A key part of the process of a child becoming emotionally intelligent is deciding what they value and what moral choices they will make, what kind of media they consume, what friends they make, and how they respond in a situation like bullying. As children internalize these values, they are ready to take a stand against what they know to be wrong and begin to exercise their voice and power for good.

Stoplight and Child Protection for Your Kids

We can't always be present in kids' lives. Even if you maximize supervision, you won't be there all the time. What we can do, though, is teach our children how they can protect themselves from potential threats and dangers around them. Understanding child protection in simple Stoplight terms can equip your children with the tools they need to stay safe.

Safe People

Red people are people you don't trust and should run away from. Yellow people are people that you may often see, but you do not yet trust. You must be cautious with these people. Green people are people that you trust and that you are completely safe around. Of course, there are instances when people that should be safe are not safe. In that case, these people are no longer Green people, they are Yellow or Red people. Help your child by making sure they are most often around Green people.

Safe Touch

Red touch includes physical or sexual abuse. When minors are sexually abused, it is often by someone they know, so they must be empowered to speak up about it. It can be very difficult to talk about being sexually abused when they don't know what the trusted adult they are disclosing it to will say. If children know that their body belongs to them, and they are told that it is okay to talk about it, their risk of being abused decreases, and should it happen, they have the language to report it. Yellow touch is any touch that makes a child uncomfortable. This includes when someone is in their personal space or touching them in a way that they don't like. Green touch is any kind of touch that makes them happy—a high-five from a friend, a hug from a parent. Teach your child what kind of touch is okay.

Safe Secrets

Red secrets are secrets where someone is getting hurt. If a child is hurt, physically or sexually, and an adult says not to tell, that is a Red secret. He or she may use threats, treats, relationships, or other means to convince the child not to tell. The child should always tell a trusted adult about Red secrets.

Yellow secrets are secrets where no one is getting physically hurt, but someone is talking negatively about others or doing something wrong. In the case of gossip, a child should walk away. However, in the case of lying or cheating, a child should tell a trusted adult.

Green secrets are good secrets. These secrets always have a definable end when it no longer will be a secret. Teach children to differentiate between the types of secrets and know what to do in each situation.

Safe Places

Red places are places where you are very unsafe. Yellow places are places where you need to be cautious and aware. Green places are places that are safe, places where we can relax and feel happy. Children should run from a Red place to a Green place or a Green person. Our goal, of course, is for our child to be in mostly Green places.

If Your Child Tells You About Abuse

Our discussion on teaching our children about abusive behavior would be incomplete without discussing the reporting of these incidents. Again, it is important to establish a trust relationship with our children, so they feel safe to talk with us about uncomfortable topics such as having experienced abuse. If our children lack a good attachment with us, they will feel unsafe and be more reluctant to discuss this serious topic with us. If our children have been abused and they realize they have been abused, they may feel shame or guilt—especially if it was sexual in nature. The perpetrator may tell them not to speak of the abuse and may use fear and shame to control them. Without a strong attachment or trust relationship with our children, therefore, they will most likely never speak to us about this important issue.

In order to break the power of the abuser, we need to educate and empower our children to speak up. Giving them a voice helps them to report abuse and lets them know that they will not be in trouble for breaking the silence. We should encourage children to be brave and report all types of abuse to someone that they trust. They should be encouraged that they will be heard and understood. They should also be confident that action will be taken. Through teaching our children about this, they should have a better knowledge of how to tell someone they trust. All of these ultimately have one goal: to make our children feel safe to discuss this difficult topic.

Steps if Your Child Tells You About Abuse
1. Stay in Green.
2. Do not show the child that you are shocked or that you don't believe them.
3. Recognize the child's bravery for coming to you about a topic that can be difficult and embarrassing.

4. Be supportive of them.
5. Listen to what they say, but do not ask leading questions. Use questions like, "Can you tell me more about that?"
6. Stress to the child that this experience is not their fault and that they are not in trouble.
7. Help the child feel safe.
8. Make sure the child knows that he/she has made the right choice by telling you.
9. Don't make any promises that you cannot keep. (For example, don't promise that you won't tell anyone.)
10. Find another Green person that would be appropriate to share this with who can assist you in finding the right resources and the help you need. (Police, therapist, pastor, doctor, etc.)
11. Keep the information as confidential as possible. Only tell people that need to know.
12. Let the child know that you will take steps to help end the abuse.
13. Report the abuse! Follow the procedure in the law.

When we were preparing to move to Africa, my son asked me, "Can you promise me that nothing bad is going to happen to me?" He had heard all the stories about poisonous snakes and frequent robberies in Africa. I told him, "I can't promise you that nothing bad is going to happen. But I can promise that God is going to be with us. He will never leave us!" We live in a world where bad things happen. But we need to remember that Jesus is the Good Shepherd. God is our guide, lighting our path. He is more powerful than evil, and we need His wisdom!

Children don't know what is right and wrong unless we teach them! We cannot assume that they know what is wrong. We need to teach them to protect themselves and stand up for their values.

But they will not know those values unless we teach and model those values! And once they understand what is right and wrong (moral identity), they can start to stand up for these values. They can be the one to stand up when someone disrespects their body or disrespects other people. I need to teach my children spiritual disciplines that can become their own as they grow. I can teach my children to value other people regardless of their appearance. I can teach them to stand up for these values!

Temptation

I like to teach children in schools about temptation by using threads. I'll ask the strongest guy to come up to the front. I wrap some thin threads around his fists and ask him to try breaking them. He breaks them easily! Then, I add more and more threads. The bundle of threads gets more and more tangled and thick. It becomes more and more difficult to break those threads. Eventually, it becomes unbreakable.

I tell the kids that the threads represent the poor choices we all make at times. In the beginning, it can seem quite easy to break free from the negative consequences of these choices. Such tiny little choices! Such weak threads! Satan makes us feel like we have a handle on things. But as we continue to make these poor choices, we add more and more threads to our bondage. We get ourselves entangled and wound up in pain and darkness, and we find that we can no longer break free!

Or at least we can't break free on our own. We need to ask God to deliver us from evil. Just as a pair of scissors can be used to cut the bundled threads, God has the power to break through the entanglement of sin in our lives!

We must teach our children to be wise with their choices. I need to help my children understand that things like hanging out with the wrong friends, telling lies, and gossiping often don't

appear to be very big at first. But these choices can become a pat-.
tern, turning into a very big deal!

The internet is an easy place to make poor choices, and kids
can find it easy to believe that what they are viewing is a secret.
It is tempting to go to places where they know they shouldn't go.
It is tempting to take the shortcut through the bad area of town.
It's tempting to gossip about friends. These are ways Satan can
take hold of anyone's life. We need to teach our children that
these things are wrong—that some choices may seem easy and
pleasurable, but the consequences can be destructive for the rest
of their lives.

We all make mistakes. Temptations come our way, and we
give into them. We gossip, lie, and find ourselves in not-so-great
situations. None of us are perfect! This is why repentance is so
crucial. When we mess up, or bad things happen, we have the
opportunity to teach our children and model asking for forgiveness from God. His grace is sufficient to cover all of our poor
choices.

Our Safety and Refuge

> He who dwells in the shelter of the Most High will abide
> in the shadow of the Almighty. I will say to the LORD,
> "My refuge and my fortress, my God, in whom I trust."
> PSALM 91:1-2

No matter what is going on around us, God is our refuge. He
is our safety. When we are faced with external dangers, we can
find our rest in Him. We are constantly bombarded with damaging messages telling us how we must define ourselves—messages
from our friends, family, children, society, and even ourselves.
These messages tell you how you must define success; they tell

you whether you are loved and what you need to do to be better. But when we understand our identity in Christ, we will be secure enough to stand firm and be a witness for God's love.

Bad things do happen. But as Christians, our safety comes from the knowledge that our God is our redeemer. He takes even the most horrible, awful events and causes good to come out of them.

Sometimes we are blessed to be able to have a glimpse of God's goodness on earth, and sometimes we just have to trust that we will understand it when we stand with God in His Kingdom. But we know God not only redeems the situation, but also gives us the strength to make it through. "Even though I walk through the valley of the shadow of death, I will fear no evil, for you are with me; your rod and your staff, they comfort me" (Psalm 23:4).

We do not have to fear our troubles. We rest assured that God will give us the strength to make it through, and then redeem the situation in the end.

STOPLIGHT REFLECTIONS

1. Think back to a time when you left your children alone, and they got into something they were not supposed to. What are some ways you can avoid these situations?

2. What kind of safeguarding methods and techniques do you have in place to protect your children from the negative influences of media? What action plan do you have in place to protect them?

3. How can you break the silence about physical and sexual abuse with your children? What kind of discussions have you had with your children about their rights and about what is inappropriate or abusive behavior?

Prayer

Loving God, thank You for the children You have entrusted to me.
Shield them, I pray, from all harm. Give them a network of good
friends and good community. May they know You, love You, and
walk each day with You, running from evil and choosing good.
As a parent, make me wise, protecting them from evil and giving
them freedom to grow into all You have made them to be.

CHAPTER 14

Releasing Our Children: Service

"I'VE GOT THE SKIP ROPE!" yelled Catherine.

"I've got the ball!" shouted Joshua.

"I have the crayons and paper!" said Rachel.

"Did anyone put the snacks and water in the car?" I called out. Finally, everyone climbed in the van. There were nine of us that day, and everyone had a purpose and an activity they liked for when we arrived at our destination—a friend's house in the village. It was going to be a long, hot day with lots of children for our kids to play with.

When we arrived, our children jumped out of the van, and within minutes Joshua and Thomas were running around with a group of boys playing ball. Catherine and a few sisters went off skipping with a group of girls. One of my girls quietly sat with a child on the veranda, simply coloring together. Many hours later, at the end of that hot, tiring day, we all climbed back in the van and began the drive home. There was so much joy in the car as everyone shared their stories from the day.

Play crosses age and culture. It brings connection and laughter. On that day, God had used our family to show His love to others while building and strengthening our relationships with our friends. It reminded me that we can love and serve together as a family. Every person in our family—from youngest to oldest—is important in that effort.

Cultivating a Greener World

I once met a mother who was living a very Red life. After hearing one of my seminars, she said, "I'll be in Green when my situation becomes Green."

Interesting observation. Is this true? I have known others in Red situations whose lives, after many years, had changed for the better in one way or another. But their children had grown up disconnected from them, or their marriage had fallen apart because they were in Red for so many years. They missed an opportunity to build into and grow their children. A three-year-old will never be three again!

Our impact on our children's development will last a lifetime. But our impact on their faith and desire to serve God is even greater. If I want to teach my children to love their neighbor as themselves, I need to start as early as possible. We might think, I'll give back to my community when my children are older, and I have more time! But there will never be a perfect age or perfect time to begin leading a life in service to others. There will always be a reason why we can't. As kids get older, there are swimming lessons and piano recitals to attend, and sports practices that get in the way and add to the busyness of life. Unless I am intentional now, it is never going to happen.

We need to model service and stewardship to our children.

I can show my children how to serve others by lending a hand to those in need—inviting the widow down the street over for dinner, offering to babysit for the single mom at church. I can teach my children stewardship by being prudent with money and encouraging efficient practices—such as being less wasteful or getting the kids involved in sensible recycling. I can teach my children that the decisions they make can have a positive or negative impact on those around them and their environment.

Dr. Michele Borba writes, "We have a serious deficit. I call it the 'Selfie Syndrome.' Today's kids are more self-absorbed than ever, and narcissism rates are up fifty-eight percent in the last thirty years."[1] We live in an increasingly self-centered society. Parents should aim to have kind children who desire to make the world a better place.

Yes, it takes practice for this to become a habit. But engaging with our communities is something we can model and do as a family.

In order to serve, I need to first be in Green. I need to be aware of my emotions and the emotions of others. Using this awareness, my child and I can control and regulate our behavior, taking steps to get to and remain in Green. Being in Green means my child is ready to connect with others by taking their perspective, truly understanding and empathizing with them. Being in Green also means my child is ready to decide about what they value, as well as what is right and wrong, creating the foundation of a strong moral identity. Then my child can recognize and control their own emotions because they understand what is right and wrong. And because my child can now see and understand where others are hurting and why, they will feel compelled to get involved and engage. They can process how to make a difference in others' lives by standing up for their own values. They become socially responsible individuals and develop their emotional intelligence as they practice their new skills with frequency.

While real life isn't always this simple—my daughter might not sleep very well and be more susceptible to flip to Red—and because the people we meet are complex individuals, it may be difficult to understand why on earth they do what they do. We can believe something one minute but feel overwhelmed and do the opposite later. Sometimes, we might feel too insignificant to make any difference at all. Many days, I find it hard to motivate myself when I look around and see so many needs, so many people I cannot help, and so many problems I cannot solve. It might seem like the world is too broken for me to fix—making it easier to choose to do nothing.

Interestingly, brain science shows that humans often live happier and healthier lives when they help others. When researchers performed brain scans of people helping others, areas of their brains related to warm and relational feelings lit up, and when those participants received help themselves, those same areas went dark.[2] Neurotransmitters—the "feel good" chemicals serotonin, dopamine, and oxytocin—are all released when we are engaged in helping others. When we help others, we help ourselves by creating the right circumstances to foster happiness. Helping others has also been linked to decreasing daily stress and feelings of depression while increasing a sense of identity and self-worth.

Love God, Love Others

Sometimes as families, we want to stay in our cocoon. It is easy to remain in that safe space where we feel comfortable. It is natural to pour all of our time and energy into our own families.

God's heart is that each of our families become a safe place where each member can grow strong in love and compassion for others, an outpost of God's love and grace in our broken world. Instead of building walls around our families, He calls us to our identity as members of God's Kingdom, carrying the realm of love and light in which we live to those around us. As our children participate with us in serving others, they will be shaped in powerful and counter-cultural pathways of compassion and respect for others.

This means that there is not a choice between serving our families and serving others, although we may feel this way as we contemplate life's daily demands. How can I make a meal for my neighbors when I barely have time to make a meal for my family? Do I have the energy to cope with the extra mess it will make in my household? Do I have the energy to deal with the special needs child at church who misbehaves? Questions like these can be talked through with our children as we decide how God is calling us to follow Him. How can all of us serve God this week? What part can each of us play? Can some of us help with cooking? How can we welcome and play with our guests? How can we help in cleaning up afterward? Together as a family, we can offer our gifts up to God as we rejoice in His gifts to us.

How we serve others as a family differs as children grow older. Serving others together can be a process of growing discernment as we hear from God. It can be challenging but will be a source of growth as we together live a great adventure in God's Kingdom! We are to live as Jesus lived—with our faces turned outward to others, tangibly sharing God's love, patience, and forgiveness. We are called to be witnesses of God's love.

The Greatest Commandment

"You shall love the Lord your God with all your heart and with all your soul and with all your mind. This is the first and greatest commandment. And a second is like it: You shall love your neighbor as yourself."

MATTHEW 22:37-39

How can I reach out to my neighbors? As a young mom, I would bake bread with my children and go out into the community looking for people in need. My family has lived in Uganda, the UK, and now Greece—but we lived the same way when we were living in Canada. Wherever we are, our children can join us in ministry. We can make meals or cards together for neighbors and look for ways to be involved and show God's love to others. Ministry opportunities can become family events.

People often ask me how my children have been affected by the life we live, especially as they shared their home and parents with our adopted kids, foster kids, and many others living in our home. My husband and I ensure that our entire family participates in discussions and prays together. We are a team! We do not just model service to others—we engage our children in the process. When we adopted three of our children ten years ago, we brought our biological kids alongside, making them a part of the discussion and prayers as we made this decision. We all felt we were called by God to pursue adoption.

As I have had the privilege of watching my older children become young adults, I know that even though it was not easy, God has used these experiences to shape our children. They were able to grow in empathy and responsibility in the process. We need to look at the long-term investment, not the short-term sacrifices, to see how God uses challenges to help each member of our family become more like Him.

As followers of Jesus, we are called to go into all the world—to share God's message of love with others. Do we inspire and teach our children to share the gospel with others? Is the gospel alive and active in our homes? Do our interactions with our neighbors communicate Christ? God has called us to love Him, love others, and share that love with all the world.

The capacity to love and serve begins in the laboratory of home life. But if family life is to escape becoming an idol, such ministry must extend beyond the boundaries of the family circle and beyond the larger circumference of familiar friends and communities.

MARJORIE THOMPSON

A Natural Outflow of God's Presence

"But you will receive power when the Holy Spirit has come upon you, and you will be my witnesses in Jerusalem and in all Judea and Samaria, and to the end of the earth."

ACTS 1:8

As parents, we seek to live responsively with God, listening to Him and letting Him shape us into His likeness. We seek to reflect God's love, acceptance, affirmation, and forgiveness to our children. We are building a place of safety in which our children can flourish and grow. We are teaching and modeling a very different narrative than that of our surrounding culture; it is the narrative that we see in Christ's own life, who walked and lived in the presence of His Father, continuing to grow and flourish as He invited others into His bounty.

To grow healthy families, we, like Jesus, must be rooted in God's family. This enables us as parents to lean gracefully and lovingly into all the challenges, surprises, sorrows, mistakes, and joys of our own families. It is God's life within us that sustains us in the challenging adventure of family life. Out of God's fullness, we invite others into our space, our time, our food, our possessions, and our acts of love. As a natural outflow of the presence of God in us, it opens us to encounter God in others and shapes us into the image of our generous and good God. For this we were made:

that we, together with our children, might partner with God in the building of His Kingdom on the earth.

Our testimony as a family flows from who we are. Our investment in our family is not in competition with our witness. We demonstrate God's love and salvation as we invite others to participate in our family, reflecting His love to others.

As parents, we will find that our children are naturally being formed to a way of life that they will carry through all of their adulthood. May we have the imagination to grow our children for the sake of others—and for the sake of the world!

STOPLIGHT REFLECTIONS

How can you and your family share the love of Christ with your neighborhood? Together, brainstorm ways that you can invite someone else into your family. Look for ways to open up your home to a child or an older person.

Prayer

Precious God, let our family become strong together in Your lovely image. Because You live in us, we will live facing outward to others. Let our love overflow to our neighbors, to the marginalized within our neighborhood, to the needy across the world. Let us be a stronghold of Your Kingdom of grace and compassion.

CHAPTER 15

The Stoplight Life

It was the middle of the night, and our little toddler was having a hard time sleeping. She fussed off and on for hours. Finally, in the early morning, my husband brought her into bed with us. Still unable to settle, she tossed and turned despite our best efforts to soothe her. She climbed all over me until she found the position she wanted—her head on top of mine! Not exactly comfortable, but a few minutes later she was asleep.

As I lay there trying to get back to sleep myself, I thought about how we, as parents, cannot just make our children sleep. We provide structure and routines. We can take them for a walk before bed to tire them out. We try to make them physically and emotionally comfortable. We can even force them to stay in bed. But we really are powerless to actually cause them to fall asleep.

There's a central truth here about parenting. We provide structure. We provide a nurturing, warm home environment. We connect with our kids in positive ways, so they feel safe, valued, and loved. Yet we cannot control their choices.

As I write this, early in the morning, I looked at the schedule for today. Later, my day will include a visit to a mental health counselor for one of my children. I am grateful for this reminder that ultimately I cannot control the outcome of my parenting.

I wish I could. I wish my children never had to struggle. I wish they would never make poor choices. I wish they didn't have to suffer lifelong consequences for those choices, but I know in my heart that I don't have control over the outcome. But I can continue to create a safe home environment, to show love and acceptance, and be the best Stoplight parent possible, so my children have the best chance to succeed.

Parents are not carpenters working with a block of wood and a set of instructions. We're not looking to create and repeat creating the same object again and again. Rather, we are gardeners. We provide the best environment possible. And we watch our little plants grow, each unique, each sending out its own leaves, blooming in its own time, with its own color and fragrance. We know we had something to do with this precious living thing, but we don't get the blame if things don't turn out exactly as we planned.

Nor all the credit if events go the other way.

Setting a Spiritual Foundation

The family is a central place for spiritual formation, the beginning of the faith journey. God created families for this purpose—to serve as safe places to learn, make mistakes, and grow spiritual roots. Although communities, churches, schools, small groups, and family friends have input into the spiritual lives of children, it is the family that is charged with this privilege and this responsibility. God tells parents to teach His ways to their children: "Talk about them when you sit at home and when you walk along the road, when you lie down and when you get up" (Deuteronomy 6:7, NIV). Family is what God put in place to pass the knowledge and love of Him on to the next generation.

This spiritual formation starts at birth. Parental love is a child's first experience of God's unconditional love. We don't wait until our children can talk to begin establishing an understanding of God. The newborn infant is placed in our arms, and we love them. It will be months before we get that first smile, and perhaps years before we see a truly sacrificial act of love on their part. Yet through all the long nights and dirty diapers and tears, we love them—giving of ourselves because of our deep unconditional love. In this way we model God's love—who loved us first before we could or would return that love.

When He taught us to pray, Jesus started with, "Our Father." He is encouraging us to equate our relationship with God to our relationship with our parents, fathers in particular. How important it is to model the characteristics of God—such as love, justice, grace, holiness, mercy, acceptance—in our homes so our children's understanding of God is rooted in life and truth.

Of course, this means that we need to make sure our own understanding of God is rooted in truth. If my understanding of God is based on fear and shame, I am not going to be able to connect with God. I can't have an intimate relationship with someone I fear. If I see God as a punitive, angry God, I will fear Him, putting me in Red Brain. If I have the idea that God will never see me as good enough, I will feel shame—and I will want to turn my face away and hide.

But, together, we seek to grow in our understanding of God. Little by little, our awareness of His incredible mercy and grace increases, and we learn how to extend that to our children. We can't and won't perfectly imitate Christ in our parenting. And that is expected. But it is important that we are constantly seeking Him fully. Then our children will start their faith journey firmly rooted in a right understanding and awareness of what God is like.

Not only do we model God's love to our children, but we also model how to return that love. Our family practices many of the spiritual disciplines that Christians through the centuries have used in their demonstration of love to God. These practices—prayer, Bible study, meditation, silence, gratitude, worship, fellowship, and confession—are means by which we learn more about God. They help us grow in our relationship with God and put ourselves in a better position to receive the God's grace.

Most nights, we gather as a family before bed and do our night-time prayers by reading through the Book of Common Prayer. We attend church together. During Lent, we fast from certain habits, foods, or media choices. Each of these disciplines is an example of behavior we intentionally take to grow our relationship with God and model that for our children.

It is so easy to give up on eating a meal as a family, especially when a screaming baby is involved, or the teenager is grumbling and being disrespectful. Yet we need to be intentional about practices such as this. Love is not easy. It can be painful, because love is walking through each other's mess.

Maybe having family prayers is not convenient some nights. It would be easy to brush them aside. It is easy to skip going to church some mornings because we feel exhausted from the week. But our feelings are not always reliable. When I don't feel like going to work, I know that I have to go anyway because there will be natural consequences if I don't. We choose to make the right choices each day despite our feelings because of the values our family has decided to live by.

So when someone is complaining about having to go to church, it may be that the best response you can give as a parent is, "Yeah, I understand how you feel. I don't want to go this morning either. But I'm choosing to do this because I love God, and I know that taking time to go and worship Him with others is a way to show my love." As we model choice when it is difficult, we instill in our children the understanding that feelings don't get to rule our behavior. The family is also the place where children first learn repentance and forgiveness. When they are young, children's moral identity is tied closely to their parents'. As they head into the teen years, more and more choices are their own to make. We can't force our choices on them, but clear values that inform family behavior day to day will more likely be ingrained.

The capacity to love and serve begins in the home. But we must be careful to not let our families become our idols—becoming self-absorbed, closed off, and disconnected from our community. This is where stewardship and social responsibility become important. I need to teach my children to have a desire to serve others outside of our family by extending our capacity to love outside of familiar circles. My family does this by serving at church and other children's ministries together. We practice hospitality—inviting strangers into our home and demonstrating kindness, generosity, and empathy.

I can also model stewardship of resources to my children, encouraging them to give generously and live wisely. How does our family reduce consumption and waste? What are our attitudes and practices with money? Do we respect other living things? Do we respect the environment and communities we encounter? Do I accept people regardless of their race or background? Do I truly love my neighbor as myself?

God's love and grace toward us are never meant to stop with us. When He blessed Abraham in Genesis 12, He said, "I will bless you and make your name great, so that you will be a blessing" (12:2). God's call to us is not to have a perfect family. It is to share the blessing of His love with others. My goal as a parent is not to have easy, quiet, obedient children. My goal is to have emotionally healthy children who are on a journey to know, love, and live for Christ.

And it is a journey. There will be good days and bad. Very Green days and very Red days. The important thing is to keep moving on this journey. These skills take practice on your part and your children's. You will mess up; your children will mess up. I encourage you not to look at the mess-ups as failures but rather as opportunities to learn—understanding and celebrating that our brains are created with the ability to learn, grow, and change; that who we are now is not who we have to be tomorrow or next year or next decade. But it takes practice and repetition. Like Paul says in Philippians 3:12, it is not that we are already perfect, but we put the past behind us and work toward the goal ahead of us. So celebrate the small successes, and choose each day to do the work and create the habits that lead us down the path toward a Greener home.

The Stoplight Approach involves understanding the science of how our brains function and seeking to let that understanding shape how we relate to, and communicate with, our children. It is a wonderful lens through which we can see ourselves and others, and adapt how we teach, train, and love. Stoplight has great insights, but it is the long, deep journey of receiving and practicing the presence of God Himself that enlivens and empowers these ideas.

As you work toward having a Green home and raising emotionally literate children may you be keenly aware of God's presence and love. May you know His calming presence in those overwhelming Red moments. May you experience His connecting presence in the stressful Yellow situations. And may you rejoice in His coaching presence as day by day you learn and grow in Green and take His love out into the world.

This is my prayer for you and your family.

Acknowledgments

I want to thank so many people who have been with me as I dreamed and researched and processed and synthesized information. So many things in my own life have changed over the course of this project!

The Stoplight Approach was created in Uganda. The first book was developed in that context, to be used in international and Ugandan schools and with the parents from those schools. Since then, my husband and family have lived in England and Canada.

Now I live in Greece. Some of my children have gone to university, and my oldest recently got married! Since then, so many people have seen Stoplight as a tool that has changed their own beliefs, and they have become passionately involved. I started this to help one international school where my children attended in Uganda. One Ugandan mom named Olivia once told me, "The Stoplight Approach is needed in all schools."

I never dreamed the Stoplight Approach would become an organization. Now, here we are, working in many countries with many people who sacrificially donate their time.

I am thankful for all the people who have helped me to develop the Stoplight Approach. First, I want to thank my family. To my husband, Mark, for being a great support and encouragement and amazing dad to our kids. You go above and beyond, not only building into our kids but accepting and investing in other children or interns who live in our home. To my children: Kendra, Jesiah, Tynan, Siarah, Braeli, Darin, and Casidee, and to Giftie, Daniel, Vasco, Ryan, Lucy, and Dani, who are not technically mine, but who are part of my family in every other way. Each one of you has taught me new and unique lessons. Thank you for putting up with my less-than-perfect parenting, for helping me put my learning into practice, and for listening to The Stoplight Song and many Stoplight stories hundreds of times.

I want to thank Marilyn Foster. As I struggled to parent my newly adopted children, Marilyn brought new ideas and techniques into my life that profoundly changed the way I parented. She introduced me to the world of brain science, helped me develop the stoplight metaphor, and taught me how a child's needs change depending on their brain state. Marilyn gives credit to the teachings of Dr. Jean Clinton, Heather Forbes, Becky Bailey, Rebecca Thompson, and Bruce Perry. Marilyn's synthesis of these ideas inspired me to learn more about brain science. I am forever grateful to Marilyn and all those who directly or indirectly influenced my understanding of the science of the brain. My life and the lives of hundreds of children and families around the world are better because of this understanding.

I want to thank Anne Jones, who has worked by my side for nearly twenty-five years. I have a deep respect for Anne, who has helped me write for so long. I am truly thankful for your faithful friendship. You saw potential in Stoplight becoming an organization and worked hard to helped create it. Thanks for all your work behind the scenes. Thanks for driving the revision of this Stoplight book and all your hours working alongside me.

I want to thank Lynn Owens, who makes our Stoplight program. She works tirelessly behind the scenes, creating illustrations and other artwork for our parent workbooks. Thank you for tackling the extra work we continue to cause you!

I am thankful for all my interns, working alongside me as they lived with our family, experiencing my life firsthand. The interns God has given me have taken up the challenge to work alongside me, someone with a writing disability, helping me express my words on paper. This is not an easy task: It takes lots of patience and a sense of humor—with lots of laughter in the process. (Otherwise, you would have given up a long time ago.)

The first version of this book was created in Uganda. The foundation and initial help to introduce Stoplight in pilot schools took an energetic team of people: Ryland Frank, Rebecca Dougan, Taylore Anstey, Katherine Bennett, Lauren Koehn, and Hannah Stoesz were instrumental in getting Stoplight off the ground and running. Their hard work, creativity, patience, and perseverance cannot be overstated! They brainstormed, wrote, trained, and worked tirelessly, particularly in the earlier stages.

I am thankful for Emily Reed, Lucas Gairns, Rachel Jones, Katie Eaton, and Emily Ham, who were part of my journey in Greece, along with Rebecca and Katherine, who joined us there. They all got to experience this season of our life in a new place, within the refugee and Greek culture.

Thank you to Annabel Bowerman for being a mentor to me, both professionally and personally, encouraging me on my spiritual journey. Thanks for walking alongside me.

I am thankful for Meredith and Kendra Long for helping me work through how the Stoplight mirrors Christ's relationship with us. You helped me to see Jesus in a new way.

Thank you to Father James McCluskey, SSC, for being influential in my spiritual journey, which is evident in my story. I'm thankful for how you challenge me to a deeper relationship with God. Thanks to Father James, Kate, and their family for reaching out to our family, showing Christ's love to us.

I am thankful for Vanguard College and the students I have in my course each year who challenge my thinking. Their assignments often inspire me and give me new ideas. I am also thankful for the Awaken Missions Team: Aaron, Chelsea, Hannah, Jessica, and Katie.

My time in Uganda was helped by The National Stoplight Team and our Uganda pilot schools. Charity, Rosemary, Sylvia, and

Angeline were on our "Home Team," helping me with all my responsibilities in the home, with kids as well as with ideas to communicate so people would understand Stoplight concepts. I am also thankful to Kenneth Hopson and Leonard, who have worked as part of our team, going many extra miles to help get books printed in Uganda.

I want to thank Lisa Mayo. She has spent many hours working alongside me, going through, evaluating, organizing, and editing my writing.

Thanks for all the people who have put time and energy into some aspect of this book: Sarah Ganger, Noémie Suter, Kate Cami, Jess Reed, Maria Said, Allison Costley, Andrea Foster, Anja Terlouw, Anne Chin, Christa Sawyer, Marilyn Foster, Shelley Leith, Pam Dougan, Peter Ekayu, Mike Broomer, Corina Patterson, Alisha Seruyange, and Barbara Chettle.

Finally, I would like to thank my parents, Bruce and Sylvia Waine, who modeled amazing gifts of hospitality and love for Jesus, and for teaching me the importance of the church family in my life as a child. I know it's been hard that we have raised seven of your grandchildren across the world, and you have missed some of those normal grandparenting moments. I am thankful you have been so supportive! You have made opportunities to be amazing grandparents—through hundreds of Skype conversations where you played with the puppets, read stories, and love the kids from far away! I appreciate the difficult and sacrificial visits you both have made to Uganda and Greece.

Notes

INTRODUCTION

1. Allison Gopnik, *The Gardener and the Carpenter: What the new science of child development tells us about the relationship between parents and children.* (St. Martin's Press, 2017)

CHAPTER 1

1. Daniel Goleman, *Social Intelligence: The revolutionary new science of human relationships.* (Bantam, 2007).
2. National Scientific Council on the Developing Child (2010). Persistent Fear and Anxiety Can Affect Young Children's Learning and Development: Working Paper No. 9. Retrieved from www.developingchild.harvard.edu.
3. Dr. Bruce Perry, cited in "Does your brain state make you smarter?" article at Lakeside therapeutic schools. Found at: https://lakesidelink.com/blog/lakeside/does-your-brain-state-make-you-smarter/
4. Heather T. Forbes and B. Bryan Post, *Beyond Consequences, Logic, and Control: A love-based approach to helping attachment challenged children with severe behaviors* (Orlando, FL: Beyond Consequences Institute, 2006).
5. Karen B. Purvis, *The Connected Child: Bring hope and healing to your adoptive family.* (New York, NY: McGraw-Hill, 2007).

CHAPTER 2

1. Jane Nelsen, *Positive Discipline: The classic guide to helping children develop self-discipline, responsibility, cooperation, and problem-solving skills* (New York: Ballantine Books, Revised Edition, 2006).
2. Heather T. Forbes, *Help for Billy: A beyond consequences approach to helping challenging children in the classroom.* (Boulder, Co: Beyond Consequences Institute, 2012).

3. Daniel Goleman, *Emotional Intelligence: Why It Can Matter More Than IQ* (New York: Random House Publishing Group, 2007).

4. Bruce D. Perry, *The Boy Who Was Raised as a Dog: And other stories from a child psychiatrist's notebook: What traumatized children can teach us about loss, love, and healing.* (New York: Basic Books, 2006).

CHAPTER 3

1. Diane Benoit, "Infant-Parent Attachment: Definition, types, antecedents, measurement and outcome" (Pulsus Group, 2004) Retrieved September 2019, from https://www.ncbi.nlm.nih.gov/pmc/articles/PMC2724160/

2. Phillip Mamalakis, *Parenting Toward the Kingdom: Orthodox principles of child-rearing* (Chesterton, IN: Ancient Faith Publishing, 2016).

3. B. Bryan Post, (2010). *From Fear to Love: Parenting difficult adopted children* (Palmyra, VA: Post Institutes and Associates, 2010).

4. Daniel J. Siegel and Tina Payne Bryson, *The Whole-Brain Child: 12 revolutionary strategies to nurture your child's developing mind* (New York: Delacorte Press, 2011)

5. Daniel J. Siegel and Tina Payne Bryson. *No-Drama Discipline: The whole-brain way to calm the chaos and nurture your child's developing mind* (Brunswick, Melbourne: Scribe Publications, 2014).

6. Gordan Neufeld and Gabor Maté, *Hold on to Your Kids: Why parents need to matter more than peers* (Toronto, ON: Vintage Canada, 2004).

CHAPTER 5

1. Forbes, *Help for Billy.*

2. Siegel and Bryson, *The Whole-Brain Child.*

3. Perry, *The Boy Who Was Raised as a Dog.*

4. Perry, *The Boy Who Was Raised as a Dog.*

CHAPTER 7

1. Ross W. Greene, *The explosive child: a new approach for understanding and parenting easily frustrated, chronically inflexible children.* (New York, NY: HarperCollins Publishers Inc, 2014).

2. Albert Mehrabian, *Nonverbal Communication,* (Chicago: Aldine-Atherton, 1972).

CHAPTER 8

1. Siegel and Bryson, *No-Drama Discipline.*

CHAPTER 11

1. Adapted from the hymn and poem "Abide in Me", by Andrew Murray, classic writer of the early 20th century.

CHAPTER 12
1. Neufeld and Maté, *Hold on to Your Kids*.

CHAPTER 14
1. Michele Borba, *Unselfie: Why empathetic kids succeed in our all-about-me world* (New York: Touchstone, 2017).
2. National Institutes of Health (2007). *Brain Imaging Reveals Joys of Giving*. Retrieved from www.nih.gov/news-events/nih-research-matters /brain-imaging-reveals-joys-giving.